MW00718746

From Death to Life

From Death to Life

We have this hope, a sure and steadfast anchor of the soul

SCOTT W. BLOCK

RESOURCE *Publications* · Eugene, Oregon

FROM DEATH TO LIFE
We have this hope, a sure and steadfast anchor of the soul

Resource Publications
A Division of Wipf and Stock Publishers
199 W. 8th Ave., Suite 3
Eugene, OR 97401
www.wipfandstock.com

ISBN 13: 978-1-60608-706-0

Manufactured in the U.S.A.

To Cora: Who told me,
"Scott, you have to write a book."

To Betty: Who dedicated me to God.

To Pat: My dear wife,
without whom none of this
would have been possible.

Contents

Introduction

*Present yourselves to God as those who have been
brought from death to life.*

ROMANS 6:13B

THERE HAVE been questions surrounding the topic of death
and resurrection for as long as I can remember. Surely these
questions have been around much longer than that, perhaps
even from the beginning of human existence.

Some curiosity and several different questions regarding
this topic of death and resurrection surfaced during my stud-
ies in seminary. These issues and questions surfaced once again
inside of me post-seminary, as pastor, because I felt challenged
by what was happening in the congregation. It was difficult to
understand what I was observing in the behaviors and beliefs of
others. The challenge was not only in attempting to put words to
what I was seeing and hearing but also in developing and work-
ing on the theological pieces of the things I was observing and
dealing with. This small treatise is an attempt to put them all together. It is a way to help bring some clarity, in a form that makes
sense, and to give a response not only to myself but to others to
understand what God is doing in these specific times.

Many of the questions come not only from my own inner
fear, insecurity, and anxiety but also from a sense of wonder-
ment and curiosity. These same fears and thoughts, by simple
observation, are also present in others as I have served them in
the office and capacity of pastor. Most of the questions, however,
have generally been centered on the topic of what happens to a
person when one dies.

For example, some of the comments and questions that have been asked of me and, of course, God, are like these:

"Does the soul or spirit actually, in reality, 'leave' the body upon death, upon the cessation of breathing?"

"Do we somehow separate or split apart thereby leaving our old body or 'flesh' in the grave while the soul goes to some geographical location called heaven or hell?"

"When you die, do you wait in heaven while you are sleeping?"

"I'm a little confused, until a short time ago I always thought you immediately went to heaven and that was such a comfort to know. I know you have to be a good Christian to get into heaven, but is there such a thing as good enough?"

To rephrase the last comment and question, perhaps it could be asked in this sense: Are the scales tipped 51 percent in my favor? But how will one know when those scales are tipped and then be comforted? When is good enough "good enough" to get into heaven? Is 51 percent my entrance fee, and how do I measure it, to know for sure? Is it simply living a Christian life, which includes attending church and asking for forgiveness for your sins? I can hardly believe that this is where deep and inner comfort lies. This is not comforting at all, rather this thinking actually increases the discomfort and becomes terrifying, not only in the mind but also in the heart.

The personal question that loomed largest in my mind was *if the soul leaves the body, why is there a resurrection*? Furthermore, if I am already in heaven because my soul goes there when I die, why would I want *this particular* body back? Please, not this body, so, no thank you. These are the invasive questions and thoughts that compelled me to dig deeper and deeper into Scripture, the writings of Martin Luther, and the Confessions of the Evangelical Lutheran Church in America.

These questions, and others like them, have profound implications, not only in my life but in others' as well. The theological implications include life, death, and eternity with the sociological (biological?) human desire of comfort.

At times, there does seem to be a sense of fear blending many different pieces of theology together. Perhaps there is a mixing of the Lutheran concept of law and gospel with some circular reasoning attached to the mixing. For example, one thought is to be good enough, meaning to do enough good "works" in order to tip the scales in one's favor, while the other thought is to be able to get to heaven immediately upon death, which one won't be able to "do" because one wasn't good enough. Therefore, there is a fear of not doing enough and a fear of not being good enough. This whole thing is perhaps a twofold fear (or more), one of not being good enough and not being able to "leave" one's body. And then, of course, a deep fear that somehow the scales were not tipped enough in your favor as an entrance guarantee. As one can see, there is much wrapped up in this thought process. Here, though, only fear and terror are present, with absolutely no comfort at all in the person posing the question or to the one experiencing grief, sorrow, and tears.

This treatise hopes to at least begin discussion and dialogue around fear and comfort about death and resurrection. The topics are varied somewhat as thoughts and ideas regarding comfort and some basic theology regarding the nature of Christ and humans, the nature of life, the nature of death, and, finally, the nature of resurrection are presented. It is my hope this will bring comfort and alleviate fear to those who are terrorized and languishing with anxiety over the death and resurrection not only of themselves but of their missed loved ones too. In this manner, being comforted, full of hope, and secure with certainty of what is to come, one is able to present oneself to God as having been brought from death to life because of the sure and steadfast anchor of the soul.

The Nature of Christ

CHRIST IS INDIVISIBLE

THE NATURE of Christ can be and generally is a difficult subject to tackle. There is no easy way to do this because Christ cannot be defined with an attached label listing all the ingredients. There is no way to put him in a closed box with a neat and tidy definition. Defining Christ does border on the attempt to control him; for when something is "known" and can be named, it is then controllable, or at least one thinks it can be controlled. However, Christ can be neither controlled nor restricted and simply cannot be, no matter how much the desire to do so. For this man is God, and, surprise, we can't control God. Bearing this in mind, though, perhaps one can begin to understand some, but not all, of what Christ is about and what Christ's nature is about. Maybe then, some light will be shed on the human nature.

Nature, being the basic character or constitution of a person, is a twofold proposition. One definition of nature is "essence,": the chemical constituency, the core or fundamental nature. Essence may be one's "soul." Another way to speak of this would be the "stuff something or someone is made of." Nature can also be one's "disposition," meaning someone's or some thing's essential character. In this way it means their personality, behavioral tendency, temperament, or outlook. One may use the language in a description of another by saying "generally he is a happy person, but today he seems blue."

Accordingly, disposition follows essence. Disposition is what someone does because their essence is what someone is. One has a certain personality and a certain tendency to behave in a particular way. Therefore he does what he is. But to narrowly and concretely define the word nature is difficult because of its naturally inherent ambiguity. To put essence and disposition against each other is attempting to split them apart as they need to remain connected. However, both of these ideas (essence and disposition can be unclear), and a blending of them, occur in the following discussions.

The most natural place to begin about the nature of Christ is to state one of the most basic theological principles of Christianity. The tenet that Jesus Christ is both God and human is something accepted as true and is a fundamental belief. And as such, he is a very unique individual; none like him have ever lived before. When we speak of or about Christ, we speak of him as an individual. He is not spoken of as two people but as one, whole, complete person. He is made up of two distinct natures, divine and human, and, as such, is an indivisible person. The natures cannot be separated. No wedge can be driven between the two. An X-ray or MRI would not show two separate images. One could not point to them and say: there is one, there is the other. Rather, there would be one image and one image alone. Simply it would be that of the God/man Jesus Christ.

The doctrine, faith, and confessions of Lutheranism do not allow for the division of the person of Christ. Nestorius (c. 386–c. 451), Archbishop of Constantinople, define nature in the sense of ousia, "substance." He distinguished precisely between the human nature and the divine nature, applying a distinction between nature (ousia) and person (hypostasis). Nestorius refused to attribute to the divine nature the human acts and sufferings of Jesus.

Nestorius is regarded as one of the principal heretics in Christology. Orthodox Christology holds that Christ has two natures, divine and human, united in one person (hypostasis). Nestorius so insisted on the full humanity of Christ's human nature that it was believed to divide him into two persons, one human and the other divine. This heresy was formally condemned at the church councils of Ephesus (431) and Chalcedon (451). Nestorianism's stress on their independent natures suggests that they are in effect two persons (hypostases), loosely joined by a moral union. In essence, Nestoriansim is the belief that Christ's nature is like two planks of wood glued together.

This idea was soundly rejected by the reformists as it was deemed to actually divide the person of Christ. Furthermore, the natures and properties are not mingled in one substance or essence. The human nature is not abolished or destroyed in the person of Jesus, nor does one nature change the other into it. Jesus is God and human, in one indivisible person.[1]

In simple understanding and faith, the divine and human natures are united in such a way they have true communion with each other. This blending does not destroy each separate item or somehow equalize them and make them something totally new that is neither one nor the other. Rather, they are blended into one person. Although imperfect, perhaps the word mixture gives a little insight into this and may be a way to view it.

However, the union and communion of the divine nature and the human nature in Jesus are far different from this. These rather simple ways and terms are used in an attempt to define this complicated and mysterious piece of theology. It is difficult and can be unclear because the mixture of the two natures in Jesus is much higher and much more mysterious than our human language can explain. The nature of Jesus simply is ineffable. But on account of this union and/or communion quality,

1. Formula of Concord (FC), Epitome 8:17, in Book of Concord (BC), 489.

one can say that God is man and man is God. This descriptive statement does not really blend the properties or natures of the divine and the human, but rather each nature retains its properties, attributes, and essence.[2]

With these two natures, Jesus acts according to his one person. As the God/man, Jesus does not act in, with, through, or according to one nature only, but in, according to, with, and through both natures, with both natures and properties acting in union and communion with each other.[3]

Jesus acts in his nature in such a way that he is, which includes, but not limited to, our king, redeemer, creator, savior, and life-giver. He acts in love, for he came to give us himself because of our sin, because of our falling away from God. For it is Jesus who suffered, died on the cross, and was raised to new and resurrected life by God for us to be forgiven, completely and wholly. Jesus so loved the world that he wanted to give new life to everyone and he accomplished this through his death and resurrection.

JESUS CHRIST DIED ON THE CROSS

Jesus died on the cross and was buried. The death that he died, he died to sin, and will not die again, ever. And he now lives to God (Rom 6:9–10). But before he lived to God, Jesus descended into hell during the three days in the tomb after his crucifixion. According to the Apostle's creed recited in worship, the words, "He (Jesus) descended into hell" are spoken. From this point many and varied questions occur. Speculative and complicated questions such as:

2. *FC, Solid Declaration (SD), 8:19* in BC, 594.
3. *FC, SD 8:46* in BC, 600.

What did Jesus do there?

What did he do in hell, and how did he interact with the devil?[4]

How did this occur?

*Was it only according to the spirit or soul or according to body **and** soul?*

Did the soul descend alone, or was the divine nature with it?[5]

Did he leave his body in the tomb and preached to the spirits in some sort of a spiritual, ghostly or ethereal form?

If so, was his body then "left behind" in the tomb while this was happening?

Did he pick up his body after he was done preaching like someone who picks up their parked car when they are done shopping?

A bit of light may be shed on these questions from some obscure verses located in 1 Peter 3:18–20. It says here that Jesus made a proclamation to the spirits in prison. This perhaps responds to the question of what Jesus did during his time in the tomb, which was the three days before he rose again to new life. But there are many pieces that must be thought about because this particular pericope doesn't give enough information on this concept. First of all, some assumptions are quickly made. The scripture text says "prison" (φυλακή; *phylakē*) and not "hell" in the original Greek language of the New Testament. Furthermore, the underlying Greek word means, "1) the act of guarding, *guarding*; 2) the act of guarding embodied in a person, *a guard or sentinel*; 3) the place where guarding is done, *prison*."[6]

But the leap is still taken and the belief without proof is taken to mean *hell*. However, with some reasoning and careful thought, what would be this prison be? It certainly would not

4. Sources and Contexts, Luther's Torgau Sermon, 248.

5. Ibid.

6. Bauer, Danker, Arndt, and Gingrich (BDAG), 1067.

be heaven as heaven cannot be conceived of as some type of prison. What else then could it be? Could it be a place where God himself keeps us "under guard," safe and secure until the resurrection? It may indeed be hell due to the fact that there is no conscious and continuous existence, or it may be the hell of those who are "lost."

Second, there is no sense of time in this passage. The scripture verses do not say explicitly *when* Christ went to the "prison." The words of 1 Peter 3:19, "in which he also went" could mean that Christ did this after he died on the cross and was buried.

It is possible for Jesus to have been resurrected in the tomb prior to his proclaiming to the spirits in prison. The reasoning for this comes from the Gospel of John 20:6–7 that reads:

> Then Simon Peter came, following him, and went into the tomb. He saw the linen wrappings lying there, and the cloth that had been on Jesus' head, not lying with the linen wrappings but rolled up in a place by itself.

Verse 7b leads to the question of how the linen wrappings were rolled up in a place by itself. How else could this have been accomplished unless Christ himself was resurrected inside the tomb and rolled up the linens?

The words of 1 Peter could also give the interpretation of a "later" date after he had fully ascended into heaven, and *then* he went and preached. Either way, it seems best to think of the resurrected Lord as the one doing the preaching, rather than these verses being about some supposed geographic location, whether prison or hell. Therefore, the Lord did this preaching in his fully raised and resurrected body, not as a separating of his divine portion and leaving the human portion lying behind in the tomb. For it must be the whole man, the whole person who descended into "hell" for only God can do that. But yet the human nature has such profound union and communion with the Son of God that it has become one, and they are not divisible.[7] That means we are to have faith and to "believe that in the entire person, God and human creature with body and soul inseparable, born of the virgin, suffered, dead and buried. Therefore I am not supposed to divide up his person but instead simply to believe that this very Christ, God and human creature in one person, descended into hell."[8] How it happened or how it occurred that at first this creature was lying in the grave and then descended into hell, it must be left alone. Simply, we cannot fathom or comprehend it.[9] Believing in him and that he did this is the chief thing.[10]

CHRIST COMES TO US

It is the nature of Christ to come to people. In the Old Testament we read that God came to Adam and Eve, personally (Gen chapters 2 and 3). God came to Cain (Gen 4), Noah (Gen 6), and others. God revealed himself to Moses (Exod 3). Moses did not go to God; rather God came to Moses and spoke directly to him through the burning bush.

In the New Testament, in the Gospel narratives, God came to Mary and Joseph. Then God came to earth in the incarnation of Jesus Christ. God came to earth as a human being, in the person of Jesus Christ. According to many different scripture texts, he appeared to thousands of people, both before and *after* the crucifixion. In the scriptures there is no text stating a person went to heaven or some other place, either in body and/or spirit, and brought Christ back here. Specifically in Proverbs 30:4 it says, "Who has ascended to heaven and come down?" More explicitly in Romans 9:6ff, the scripture plainly states: "Do not say in your heart, Who will ascend into heaven? (That is, to bring Christ

7. *FC, Epitome 8:13* in BC, 488.

8. Sources and Contexts, Luther's Torgau Sermon, 248.

9. Ibid., 249.

10. Ibid.

down) or Who will descend into the abyss? (That is to bring Christ up from the dead.)" Here, plainly and simply it is stated that humans can do neither. No one can nor is able to go up/ascend to some place (where, heaven?). Likewise, no one can go down/descend to a different place (where, Hell, Gehenna, Sheol, or the Pit?). Take for example, King David, the celebrated king of the Jewish community. When he died, he did not go anywhere except to the grave. In Luke's book, Acts 2:29, it states "David is both dead and buried, and his sepulcher is with us unto this day." Then a bit further in verse 34, "For David is not ascended into the heavens." Clearly, David is nowhere except in the grave.

Christ appeared to many people in the Bible and he still comes to people today. After Christ was crucified and raised from the dead by the Father, he sent the Holy Spirit to us, and where God and the Spirit are, there is Jesus. Likewise, where the Spirit is, there is Jesus and God. This is how, in John 3:13, Christ was able to have said: "No one has ascended into heaven except the one who descended from heaven, the Son of Man." (The Son of Man is a title that Christ uses when speaking about himself.) Jesus also said, "Where I am going you cannot come" (John 8:21). Jesus tells us in simple and ordinary language, you cannot come.

Come. Sent. Ascend/Descend. There is a definite direction. No one goes to God. God is doing the work, God is the one with the direction, moving to us, coming toward us, joining with us, and dwelling in us.

The direction, the movement that scripture tells us about, is a one-way street. Christ comes to us, to you and me; we do not go to Christ. Christ has opened the door to God for us, because he is the first fruits, meaning the first person of the resurrected dead (1 Cor 15:20). Christ comes to us and, because he does, we are able to have a relationship with him. We cannot go, like in splitting or separating from our body, to Christ to have a relationship. We have this wonderful relationship with the living God, Jesus Christ, because he first loved us and came to us. He has called us and enlightened us through the Gospel. Christ does all the work and we reap the benefits. We passively receive gracious gifts that come as a result of this relationship. This relationship is unlike any other, especially any other that we now have with other human beings.

Today, the action or the motion is still one way. It is Christ who comes to us in and through faith, the Holy Sacrament of Baptism, and in spirit. He comes to us in the Holy Sacrament of Communion. These are where we have received the Holy Spirit in baptism and we receive the body and blood of Christ in communion. Christ is present at the right hand of the majesty of God, in heaven, and Christ can also be present wherever he wills and he is present with the church and community on earth. He is present not in part or in only one-half of the person but in the entire person in both natures and is wholly and completely present.[11]

CHRIST COMES TO US TO DWELL IN US

It is the nature of Christ to come to us. It is Christ's nature to dwell among us. Here are but a few examples of scripture verses supporting Christ's being among us:

EXODUS 29:45
I will dwell among the Israelites,
and I will be their God.

DEUTERONOMY 12:11A
. . . then you shall bring everything that I command
you to the place that the Lord your God will choose as
a dwelling for his name:

DEUTERONOMY 14:23A:
in the presence of the LORD your God, in the place
that he will choose as a dwelling for his name,

11. *FC, SD 8:78* in BC, 607.

DEUTERONOMY 16:2B:
at the place that the LORD will choose as a dwelling for his name.

2 CHRONICLES 29:6B:
they have forsaken him, and have turned away their faces from the dwelling of the LORD,

JEREMIAH 7:3:
Thus says the LORD of hosts, the God of Israel: Amend your ways and you doings, and let me dwell with you in this place.

EZEKIEL 37:27:
My dwelling place shall be with them; and I will be their God, and they shall be my people.

Virtually the entire book of Exodus tells about the living God dwelling among the Israelites in the Tabernacle. Meanwhile, the New Testament books describe the life of Christ dwelling among not only the Jews but among the Gentiles as well. God most definitely wants to be around and chooses to dwell among people.

It is also Christ's nature to dwell in us. Christ is in you and he lives in your heart and dwells in you. There are many scripture verses regarding this. Following are but a few quotations:

ISAIAH 57:15:
For thus says the high and lofty one who inhabits eternity, whose name is Holy: I dwell in the high and holy place, and also with those who are contrite and humble in spirit, to revive the spirit of the humble, and to revive the heart of the contrite.

ROMANS 8:9–11:

But you are not in the flesh; you are in the Spirit, since the Spirit of God dwells in you. Anyone who does not have the Spirit of Christ does not belong to him. But if Christ is in you, though the body is dead because of sin, the Spirit is life because of righteousness. If the Spirit of him who raised Jesus from the dead dwells in you, he who raised Christ from the dead will give life to your mortal bodies also through his Spirit that dwells in you.

1 CORINTHIANS 3:16:

Do you not know that you are God's temple and that God's Spirit dwells in you?

2 CORINTHIANS 12:9B:

So, I will boast all the more gladly of my weaknesses, so that the power of Christ may dwell in me.

2 CORINTHIANS 13:5B:

Do you not realize that Jesus Christ is in you?

EPHESIANS 3:17:

And that Christ may dwell in your hearts through faith, as you are being rooted and grounded in love.

JAMES 4:5:

Or do you suppose that it is for nothing that the scripture says, "God yearns jealously for the spirit that he has made to dwell in us"?

REVELATION 21:3:

And I heard a loud voice from the throne saying, "See, the home of God is among mortals. He will dwell with them as their God; they will be his peoples, and God himself will be with them . . ."

It makes sense then as the Bible tells us Jesus wants to dwell among us, dwell in us, that he would also want to gather us up like a hen gathers up the brood (Matt 23:37). This will be the resurrection where and when Christ has finally come to all of us, has finally come to take us all home, and has finally and completely gathered all of his faithful followers totally together. He gathers us all so that he may be all in all. Scripture tells us that:

COLOSSIANS 3:11:
In that renewal there is no longer Greek and Jew, circumcised and uncircumcised, barbarian, Scythian, slave and free; but Christ is all and in all!

1 CORINTHIANS 15:28:
When all things are subjected to him, then the Son himself will also be subjected to the one who put all things in subjection under him, so that God may be all in all.

EPHESIANS 1:23:
Which is his body, the fullness of him who fills all in all.

EPHESIANS 4:6:
One God and Father of all, who is above all and through all and in all.

2

The Nature of Humans

To describe and define the nature of humans is a wide and varied task simply because humans are wide and varied. As humans, we love, we hate, we sleep, eat, breathe, walk, drink, talk, think, smile, laugh, have feelings, and on and on. Like many things in life, there is not always a narrow definition. There are things we can do and there are things we cannot do. As humans there are some things about us that cannot be changed.

As humans, we are subject to many things during our stay on the planet we call home. We are acted upon by the elements of weather, hot, cold, rain, snow, and so on. People are also subject to mental/emotional responses of feelings as well as physical bodily functions such as hunger and thirst. These things are not only "life" but our nature as well.

We are subject to the law. This is not only the law of humans that tells us to stop at stop signs, file your income tax, and whatever goes up must come down. The law is also the divine law of God, known commonly as the Ten Commandments plus all the other requirements laid out in the Old Testament. In the New Testament, Christ "increases" the law and adds more requirements to it as well. These things we are supposed to do, are required to do, indeed, *must do* in life if we are to live and to love and serve God and the neighbor. We are to live up to these ten laws and obey them, thereby fulfilling and completing them.

But it is in our nature to rebel. At times, we refuse to do what has been required by human law. Many more times we refuse to do what has been divinely commanded by God. This is a twofold problem for us because not only are we unable to fulfill the law, we simply don't. Our nature is as the apostle Paul said in his letter to the Romans. No one can describe our inner conflict and inner nature better than this:

> For we know that the law is spiritual; but I am of the flesh, sold into slavery under sin. *I do not understand my own actions. For I do not do what I want, but I do the very thing I hate.* Now if I do what I do not want, I agree that the law is good. But in fact it is no longer I that do it, but sin that dwells within me. *For I know that nothing good dwells within me, that is, in my flesh. I can will what is right, but I cannot do it. For I do not do the good I want, but the evil I do not want is what I do.* Now if I do what I do not want, it is no longer I that do it, but sin that dwells within me. So I find it to be a law that when I want to do what is good, evil lies close at hand. For I delight in the law of God in my inmost self, but I see in my members another law at war with the law of my mind, making me captive to the law of sin that dwells in my members. Wretched man that I am! Who will rescue me from this body of death? Thanks be to God through Jesus Christ our Lord! So then, with my mind I am a slave to the law of God, but with my flesh I am a slave to the law of sin.[1]
> *(Emphasis added)*

We are subject to trouble in this life (1 Pet 4:17). We are subject to sin that we bring upon ourselves. We are subject to sin that is brought upon us following in the steps of our ancestors by something called original sin. It is original sin that corrupts our nature. This sin is not a slight corruption of our nature, but it is a deep corruption that nothing that we deem good has survived in either our body or our soul. No one except God alone is able to

---

1. *The Holy Bible: NRSV.* 1989 (Rom 7:14–25).

separate the corruption of our nature from our nature itself. This separating will take place by way of death in the resurrection.[2]

This sin then makes us subject to death. All of us are mortal, and all of us have died (2 Cor 5:14). As mortal in our nature, we, under the sentence of death, have indeed received that sentence of death (2 Cor 1:9). We are then dead because of sin (Rom 8:10). Being mortal and dead, we should not think of ourselves more highly than we ought but to think with sober judgment (Rom 12:3). This all means that we are not God. How could we be, since we are dead?

As mortal and as human beings, we have no inherent true or genuine power. Can anyone you know by worrying or some other method or process, whether internal or external, add even a single hour to their span of life (Matt 6:27)? Furthermore, one should not make any promises to another, for one cannot make even one little hair white or black (Matt 5:36). We have no powers to gain life. We have no power to get to heaven, we cannot go there of our own volition. We may "will" it, but we are unable to do it. Just as it is beyond the power of a person who is physically dead to prepare or make something happen in oneself, or in the world to regain one's own life on earth, neither is it possible by one's own power to obtain spiritual and heavenly righteousness from God. This is not possible unless God has liberated sin from that person and made them alive.[3]

HUMANS WANT AND NEED COMFORT

With regard to the previous discussion, one can understand our dilemma. Although the preceding was perhaps heavy and discouraging because it took away all of our power and what we think we are, there is one thing that can be brought forward and

2. Formula of Concord (FC), *Epitome 1:59,* in Book of Concord (BC), 466–67.

3. FC, Solid Declaration (SD) 2:11, in BC 522.

discussed relating to the nature of the human species. And that one universal thing is that humans *want* and *need comfort*. Who wouldn't want and need comfort knowing that we are dead even though we are alive and have no power? The need to desire comfort is simply built into us. It is due to the nature of the life we live and to the things we are "subjected." We want comfort and to be comforted from all the scariness, uncertainty, anxiety, and fear in life. Not only do we want comfort in life, but we want comfort in death too. There was a psychologist who said what humans need in life are three things: food, shelter, and clothing. Simply stated, those three things all bring comfort.

This idea of comfort is present in many facets and aspects of people's lives, but nowhere is it more visible than at a funeral. Comfort is also required in funeral homes, hospital rooms, emergency rooms, intensive care units, and nursing homes. These different settings require comfort at different levels.

In these various places and situations, when death is present, people speak of "leaving." Direct statements like "I know they are in a better place" have been spoken and heard. When someone is very near to death, one may say, "I know they are not there anymore, they have already left." They seem to think that somehow the soul has shed its prison and is now free floating. It is like the soul has left the building. It seems that many, many people believe that this "separation" of body and soul happens, and it happens at the "moment" of death.

The idea of the soul "splitting off" or leaving the body at the moment of death stems from the inner human desire of needing and wanting comfort. The living person watching their loved one suffering immensely in the last hours and minutes of the throes and pangs of death simply cannot stand the torment their family member is experiencing. Then, when that person dies, the survivors, who deeply loved the deceased, cannot bear to think of their loved one as dead, in the ground, and decaying. They cannot think of them as cold, in the casket, in the winter, and lying alone in the grave. This situation is too awful and quite painful. To comfort themselves they believe and think the soul/spirit has "departed" and gone to God. Or perhaps it has gone to God in heaven in all its faculties and in all its senses, except without its fleshly and earthly body, leaving the suffering part behind. In the minds of the survivors, this ends the suffering of the person who is dying and it becomes easier to bear for those who are left behind. "Knowing" this brings some comfort to the bereaved.

But this comfort can be, and often is, shallow and fleeting, because it is this type of comfort that we are trying to make inside of ourselves. Humans, in and of their own power, want to take care of themselves and want do it alone. However, human beings have great difficulty in doing this one simple thing of self-comfort. In fact, it may be quite impossible. One cannot "make" comfort inside of oneself. To even attempt to do this a way must be found to measure the amount of comfort that one already possesses. How does one do that? One must then decide to make more of it, that is, whatever the material that comfort is made of. Then say to yourself, "Make more comfort" and, somehow, it is done. When more material is made, one knows it and the amount of comfort one manufactured can be compared to the previous amount one possessed. This appears to be quite an uncertain and rather unlikely task to accomplish even with the most immense effort.

Certainly some small things are comforting, such as eating "comfort food." This can provide some solace, depending on the circumstances requiring the comfort, but it is short lived. Surely this will not help when one is grieving over a death. True, deep, and eternal comfort comes only from Christ. This comfort is peaceful and joyful and cannot be knocked out of a heart by external circumstances. Perhaps this is why theology and Christ are pushed to the end, because we know that it is Christ alone who brings such great peace.

Interestingly, it is quite doubtful one has ever expressed the thought that a loved one has gone to "hell." Neither has anyone said they know their loved one is in a "worse place" as opposed to a "better place." Even though the deceased may have been acknowledged as someone who was a bit edgy, mean or angry, uncaring and not very nice at times, or perhaps not very generous, and if there were some familial problems, never has anyone said they thought their loved one was in hell or has gone to the devil. This, of course, would not be comforting for anyone to hear, think, or feel.

The idea of comfort is especially evident and particularly visible when a child dies, or when someone dies violently and/or unexpectedly, such as in a car accident. At the funeral of a three-year old who was killed in an accident, the pastor preached this particular child was now sitting on the lap of Jesus in heaven. Another person at the funeral said they thought Jesus was playing "monster trucks" with the child. The death of a child is almost unbearable because it is extremely painful in heart and mind. The thought of that young child, alone in the grave, cold, and dead, is more than one can bear. So comfort is required, needed, and wanted to assuage the deep grief, pain, and suffering.

When a person who is quite elderly dies, it appears less comfort is required by the bereaved. For example, take the uneventful death of a ninety-eight-year-old man. Perhaps he just "drifted off" and went to sleep. At this type of funeral, people are lighter, more jovial, and have more laughter than tears. The family members appear quite comforted because the longevity of life of the deceased somehow makes the situation better, more tolerable, and more acceptable. When the deceased has lived a "long and happy life," this type of death is much easier to handle and deal with. In such an instance, one would not hear the phrase that the deceased is "sitting on the lap of Jesus." The family somehow has enough "inner" comfort to handle this particular situation.

It seems that living a long and happy life does not push one's theology to the end.

There is a correlation between the age of the person and the amount of comfort required. Simply speaking, the younger the person, the more comfort required while the converse is the older the person, the less comfort required. These statements are not readily quantifiable and there is no empirical scientific data or information available. However, in virtually all of these many and varied situations, the language is still that of "leaving" and "going to a better place."

When an aunt of mine died a number of years ago, I attended the funeral as a nephew and not as the presiding clergy. As I listened to the pastor preach, he offered some words of what he thought was comfort to a grieving family. In the sermon, he said he "knew she was sitting up in heaven playing cards." In one small aspect, the preacher was right, for my aunt was an avid card player. In reality though, his statement was not at all comforting to me, not the least little bit, as it was difficult to imagine or to think of heaven as a dimly lit and smoky room, where a small, bare, single light bulb hung from a frayed wire above where my aunt was sitting at a small, round table, wearing a green plastic visor, playing cards with some relatives who had died before her. Where was Christ in the sermon? Why was Christ not preached as the only one who brings comfort? Why was he not even offered as comfort? Where was Christ in the situation the pastor described? Perhaps he was the dealer and wearing a green visor too? How is this style of preaching comforting for anyone?

COMFORT, MARTIN LUTHER STYLE

Even the great reformer Martin Luther (1483–1546) himself needed comfort differently when someone close to him died. Under these times of stress and duress, he, too, sought Christ and pushed his personal theology toward that end. Here we read of some differences in his thought, his verbal expressions, and his theology when he is offering comfort to others than when he himself needed it.

One can see the development of his theological thought through the years as he offered advice and gave comfort and words of consolation to his friends and family. But when people especially close to him died, notice that the theology he clung to so tightly went right out the window when death struck very close to home. This happened to him because of the depth of pain that he suffered. Luther, like many of us today, made the "leap" due to the extreme duress. Extreme suffering and grief require comfort, and the best comfort is to think that the loved one has "left" and is "sitting on the lap of Jesus" with all their faculties, rejoicing with all their lost relatives, lost friends, and perhaps their lost immediate family.

Luther wrote numerous letters over his lifetime and many of these are extant so we are able to peek into Luther's public and not-so-private life. He communicated with friends, family, educators, kings, and princes. The following letters are in chronological order.

To Queen Mary of Hungary, whose husband had died (1526), Luther wrote to her to comfort and console her:

> …still much consolation is to be found in the scriptures, and especially in the psalms, which abundantly point to the dear and gracious Father and Son in whom sure and everlasting life lies hidden.[4]

This is a portion of a letter to Thomas Zink and his wife (1526) to whom Luther wrote to console them when their son, John, died after an illness:

> But let this be your best comfort, as it is ours, that he fell asleep (rather than departed) decently and softly with such a fine testimony of his faith on his lips that we all

4. Luther, Martin, *Luther: Letters of Spiritual Counsel*, 58.

> marveled. ... Saint Paul says that we should not mourn over the departed, over those who have fallen asleep, like the heathen.[5]

In a letter to his own dear father, John Luther, who was seriously ill in 1530 and died about three months after receiving his son's letter, Martin wrote:

> The longer a man lives, the more sin and wickedness and plague and sorrow he sees and feels. Nor is there respite or cessation this side of the grave. Beyond is repose, and we can then sleep in the rest Christ gives us until he comes again to wake us with joy.[6]

And then after his father died on May 29, 1530, Luther wrote to his friend Philip Melanchthon on June 5, 1530 and said:

> This death has cast me into deep mourning, not only because of the ties of nature but also because it was through his sweet love to me that my Creator endowed me with all that I am and have. Although it is consoling to me that, as he writes, my father fell asleep softly and strong in his faith in Christ ...[7]

Luther wrote to Mr. and Mrs. Knudsen (1531) to comfort them when their son died. Not much is known about the boy's death, but the letter in its entirety suggests it was an illness of some duration:

> So you too, when you have mourned and wept moderately, should be comforted again. Indeed, you should joyfully thank God that your son had such a good end and that he has gone to sleep in Christ so peacefully that

5. Ibid., 65.
6. Ibid., 32.
7. Ibid., 30.

> there can be no doubt that he is sleeping sweetly and
> softly in the eternal rest of Christ.[8]

This next quote comes from the book *Table Talk,* which is one of the volumes of Luther's Works (WA, TR, V, No. 6445). It was recorded by Anthony Lauterbach in 1537 and is reprinted in *Letters of Spiritual Counsel.* Luther here is speaking to the aunt of Catherine von Bora (Luther's wife). The aunt was a beloved member of the household and cared for and helped raise Catherine and Martin's children. This is an account of Luther's last ministry to her before she died:

> You will not die but will fall asleep like an infant in a
> cradle, when morning dawns, you will rise again and
> live forever.[9]

Luther wrote to Catherine Metzler in 1539 to help her and offer comforting words. Her husband, John, died in October and then her son, Kilian, died in December of the same year. According to the letter, the son was only sick for nine days and then died. The letter said, "At first he had jaundice, which is not fatal … Then colic set in, and this in turn was followed by epilepsy, which he was not able to overcome since he was by nature very frail." Luther wrote:

> This too should comfort you, that your son was a well-
> behaved and godly boy, a good Christian who had a
> blessed departure from this wretched world … But your
> son is with the Lord Christ, in whom he fell asleep.[10]

In 1541, Luther wrote to Frederick Myconius, a pastor, who was suffering from a pulmonary infection that later turned into symptoms of tuberculosis. He recovered from these illnesses and

8. Ibid., 61.
9. Ibid., 46.
10. Ibid., 73.

died about five years later. However, he thought he was close to death when Luther wrote to comfort him:

> I received your letter in which you report that you are sick unto death that is, if you interpret it rightly and spiritually, sick unto life. I was singularly pleased to learn that you are unafraid of death, of that sleep which is the common destiny of all good men, and that you rather desire to depart and be with Christ.[11]

The Luther family had a close relationship with the Jonas family. So the news of the death of Catherine (1542), Justin Jonas's wife, came as a shock. The death came suddenly, presumably as a result of complications connected with childbirth. It is unclear whether the child survived or not. It is also in this letter that we get a hint of Luther's grief as he spoke about his own daughter:

> This you cannot doubt, for she fell asleep on Jesus' bosom with so many godly and blessed expressions of faith in him. It was in this way that my daughter also fell asleep, and this is my great and only consolation.[12]

The first letter quoted in this section is from 1526 and this *Table Talk* (LW, 5494, Vol. 54:430) quote is from September 1542, sixteen years later. It reveals Luther's "change" when comforting himself and his wife, as opposed to the care, consolation, and comfort he offered others. Furthermore, there is just *something inexpressible* about a child getting sick and dying rather than a parent or a spouse, or even oneself:

> Afterward he said to his daughter, who was dying in bed (d. September 20, 1542), "Dear Magdalene, my little daughter, you would be glad to stay here with me, your father. Are you also glad to go to your Father in heaven?"

11. Ibid., 47.
12. Ibid., 76.

> When his wife wept loudly, Martin Luther comforted
> her by saying: "Remember where she is going. It will be
> well with her. The flesh dies but the spirit lives."[13]

In this letter of 1544, Luther had the sad task of informing
George Hoesel of the death of his son, Jerome Hoesel, who took
sick with a fever, died, and was buried the next day:

> inasmuch as Christ indicates that "in heaven their an-
> gels do always behold the face of my Father which is in
> heaven," you must have no doubt that your son is rejoic-
> ing with our Saviour, Christ, and with all the saints. I too
> am a father, and I have lived to see several of my own
> children die. I have also experienced other adversities
> which are worse than death. I know that these things
> are painful.[14]

This may be the toughest letter written by Luther. He wrote
to a man named Andrew Osiander in 1545. Andrew's first wife
died and he remarried. Then Andrew's second wife, Helen, died
about the same time as did a daughter from his first marriage.
This double tragedy evoked these consoling words from Luther:

> I know from the death of my own dearest child how
> great must be your grief. It may appear strange, but I
> am still mourning the death of my dear Madgalene, and
> I am not able to forget her. Yet I know surely that she is
> in heaven, that she has eternal life there, and that God
> has thereby given me a true token of his love in hav-
> ing, even while I live, taken my flesh and blood to his
> Fatherly heart.[15]

Here stands Luther, comforting and consoling others, while
he himself is still grieving and hurting. It seems he grieved for at

13. Ibid., 50–51.
14. Ibid., 79.
15. Ibid., 80–81.

least three years over the loss of his daughter. As his pain grew worse over time, he had to learn how to cope and he desired to be comforted himself. We see that the language he used in comforting others changed from "life lies hidden" and "fell asleep" to words like "go to your Father in heaven" and "your son is rejoicing with all the saints." The sense that is portrayed in these letters and in the progression of Luther's maturing theology and his own inner self is this: According to the level and depth of the pain that one feels, the level and depth of comfort required is more than one feels in the distress, in order to displace or replace the "bad" feelings with the "good" ones. Using a bad analogy, consider a glass filled to the brim with water. This represents the degree of discomfort one is feeling. In order to rid oneself of this discomfort, one must be comforted with at least the same amount of comfort as there is discomfort. But this only makes the playing field level. More comfort than discomfort is required in order to feel comforted and have relief. Therefore, more water must be poured into the glass, overflowing, spilling out, and over the brim until there is none of the original discomfort left. It is likewise with people's own "personal" theology. In order for someone to feel comforted because of extreme duress, they simply *must* push their theology to the end, filling it up to the brim, pushing out all the bad, and having only the best remain, which is that their loved one has gone to God in heaven and is "playing cards" or "sitting on the lap of Jesus."

3

The Nature of Life

THE APOSTLE Paul in 1 Corinthians 15:31 said "I die every day." What a tough life he must have had. We have no sense of this in the world of today, at least not in the United States. What a tough life he must have lived, being whipped, stoned, beaten, and shipwrecked, and all of them numerous times. Nevertheless, and unbelievably, he hoped. He hoped for the life coming rather than for the one he already possessed. This is the hope of the life coming back to us that we have lost through sin. Although one really wouldn't want to call the life we have here on earth a death, in reality, it is a continuous journey toward death. From the moment of our birth, we begin to die. But through baptism we are restored to a life of hope, or rather a hope of life. This is the true life, which is lived before God.[1]

Life on earth is a life of faith. It is not always easy but it is the assurance of things hoped for (Heb 11:1). One must live in the hope of Christ, for there is nothing else to trust, to hang on to, or to rely on. Nothing made of human hands is reliable enough, strong enough, powerful enough, or enduring enough to hang on to. Nothing else measures up. There is nothing to trust in but Christ, for there is nothing else to trust in because everything else in this life is temporal, fleeting, and not lasting. The things of the world are eaten away by moths and if not eaten, then it corrodes under rust (Matt 6:19–20). But when that is understood and your life is lived in this *particular* faith, then life *is* the fullest

1. *Luther's Works (LW)* 1:196.

and richest that one could only dream about. Rather than having nothing in life, one now has everything. But this faith is not an easy thing. It is not human power but divine power that makes us alive and makes life worth living. Through faith, even though we know we will die (Eccl 9:1–10) and we sit in the shadow of death (Ps 23:4, Matt 4:16), light has dawned. Faith, given to us by Christ himself, enables us to overcome sin, death, and the devil. This faith is a new life, producing new impulses and new works.[2] It brings the Holy Spirit into our hearts and deeply into our lives. This life is a relationship with the resurrected and living Lord and this is where everything exists. This is the bottom line. This is where life is not death, but new life, new hope, and hope for new eternal life. In Christ they all come together and make this life on earth worth living.

The life lived is a delight in God. Our life overflows with happiness, joy, and peace, for life is a joyful thing full of pleasure and delight. For the Bible tells us to "Take delight in the Lord and he will give you the desires of your heart." [3] When one knows Christ and loves God with their whole heart, the ways of life are pleasant, and the paths of God are peace. God is no longer to be feared. We are neither driven by duty or service, nor are we in bondage to our profession. Serving others, serving our neighbors becomes pleasurable; it is sheer happiness and delight. These things are all done unhindered, without compulsion and coercion, and with sheer joy.

There is no longer the time to be under law, but rather to be under grace in this life. There is freedom by a radical grace through faith in Christ. Even though humans are imperfect and unworthy, they are acceptable to God through this faith. We are made "right" with God and are no longer afraid. This life is pleasing to God, a delight, and life is lived spontaneously from the

2. *Augsburg Confession (CA), Apology,* 4:250, in *Book of Concord (BC)* 143.

3. *The Holy Bible: NRSV*, Psalm 37:4.

heart, renewed by the Holy Spirit. But sin is still present and we sin in thought, word, and deed. We struggle and we suffer until we die. But then sin is put off, it is "killed," and we will be completely renewed in the resurrection.[4]

Our lives begin in Baptism, which is the death of the old. Perhaps one could say, although not totally correctly, that baptism is the beginning, life is the middle, and death is the end, at least of our physical body. This is the "journey" of life, to move from death into life. In baptism, we have received the spirit of Christ and Christ dwells in our hearts during this life on earth and the next. We have been baptized into the death of Christ, and as Christ was raised so will we be (Rom 6:34). Our life and lives come from every word that comes from the mouth of God (Matt 4:4). Our lives consist of the dwelling of God in our hearts and the words from God. Therefore it is Christ who makes us alive, not only here on this planet, but in the future, the life to come, the hope of all hopes. We can depend on this because it is God's work and God's words, and not our own. Therefore one can both lie down and sleep in peace (Ps 4:8) now, today, and when death comes, for God is a sovereign God. In Romans 9:16, all things depend on God and not on human will or exertion, for God shows mercy. That is our trust, our hope, and our very life, for God keeps watch over our soul (Prov 24:12). Surely there is a future, and hope will not be cut off (Proverbs 23:18). These are sure and certain words of comfort and hope. This is our steadfast anchor of the soul.

4. Formula of Concord (FC), Solid Declaration (SD) 6:225, in BC, 567–68.

4

The Nature of Death

THE NATURE OF PHYSICAL DEATH

WHAT IS the nature of death? How is it that one thinks about the nature of something indescribable, uncontrollable, unwanted, and most of the time acts like a thief? Death can be painful or not, sudden or not, and it comes in many and varied ways. Yet we all experience death in some manner of various degrees at different points in our lives.

As death is unavoidable, most of us want to live in denial. In denial, one can *avoid* death and pretend it does not exist. Another way to avoid death is to *escape* it by having our soul split off from the body, thereby not having to experience death. We escape prior to the actual moment of death. But this thinking and wishing simply doesn't work, especially in receiving comfort that lasts. Denial may work for a while, helping us in some small manner, but then death walks right up, looks at us eye to eye and face to face, which snaps us back to reality. There is not much comfort there.

Many, if not all, have had someone close die. Some of us have died emotionally; some have died to ourselves; and *all* of us will physically die at the end of our life, when our breathing stops once and for all. The exception, of course, is to be alive at the time of the second coming of Christ.

Death occurs at several levels. There is the death of the organism, a person as a whole, which is usually preceded by the death of individual organs, cells, and parts of cells. The death we recognize is marked by the cessation of heartbeat, respiration, movement, and then brain activity. The precise time of "somatic" (Greek, soma, meaning body) death can at times be difficult to determine.

After death, some changes occur in the body that determine time and circumstances of death. Organs of the body die at different rates. At death, the body cools down, influenced by the ambient temperature of the environment. Stiffening of the muscles begins about five to ten hours after death and disappears in three or four days.

Many ideas about what constitutes death vary with cultures and their beliefs. Most people in this country believe that death has occurred when vital functions such as breathing and circulation cease. This belief has now been challenged because many lives can be sustained through medical and mechanical means. Therefore many now view brain inactivity as the sign that death has occurred. This brings to light the related issues of defining the criteria for death, rights of the dying, and delving deeper and deeper into judgmental, ethical, and moral issues far beyond this discussion.

THE NATURE OF "SPIRITUAL" DEATH

The question about what happens to a person physically, meaning to the physical body, was answered above. Many people recognize and understand these things. But many more are interested in and curious about what happens "spiritually." This is the point where one's theology is pushed to the end. It is what happens when someone near and dear to us dies, meaning one "leaves," "goes to heaven," or "sits on the lap of Jesus." Even though we desperately want it, we desperately need it, and we even try to "will" it that is not necessarily what happens to us at the end of our life, that is, when our breathing stops.

There is a movie entitled *The Final Inquiry* and in it one of the characters says, "I've always been curious about the beyond because I fear nothingness." This is what many, if not all, of us fear. Perhaps this notion is another aspect of what pushes our theology to the end. Fear of death, fear of nothingness, fear of not living on in continuity all contribute to not having comfort and being comforted. It is a driving force that pushes it all to the end. The end being God, because there is nothing beyond or past that, as God *is* the end. What is beyond that? What is beyond God? Not even an active imagination can bring up something past or beyond God.

Under certain circumstances, especially surrounding and regarding death, people react. They react emotionally. The forces of emotions disrupt values, reason, and the ability to make decisions. The emotion of passion interferes with judgment. All of this then gives way to unremitting anxiety. The best theology, even if is exceedingly clear and very sound, helps little when people are under such an emotional stress. Under this type of duress our thinking brain gives way to the lower, more automatic brain known as the "reptilian." This is where the notion of the "fight or flight" response comes into play that we all have experienced. In this state, good theology as well as good sense are suspended.[1] This is how one's personal theology gets pushed, and pushed hard, even though it is not correct. It is from this stress that the beliefs of splitting apart, or going someplace, or sitting on the lap of Jesus come into play. We hold onto this belief even after the time of grieving has passed simply to hold onto the comfort this thinking brings. Then we can apply this belief again when death strikes at us.

Away from the stress and anxiety of death, away from the hospitals, nursing homes, and intensive care units and with no

1. Peter Steinke, *Healthy Congregations*, 86.

loved one imminently dying, our emotions settle down and our brain comes out of the fight or flight response. Because no comfort is being required at this particular moment in time, one can think clearly and rationally, using the "higher" brain and not be driven by emotions or reactions.

So let us lean on and think rationally about what the Holy Bible has to say and teach us regarding death. In this way we are removed from the situation emotionally and keep at least some of our own bias out of the discussion. We lean on scripture, the Holy Bible, God's Word, because this is the authority of life and death. This is not an attempt to twist the words of the Bible by use of proof texting. Rather one reads scripture of how we fit into it and how it interprets us, not the other way around. This means to read about what the word of God is saying and speaking to me, about me and my life, and how one must adjust one's life to it.

The following reasons are in support of the suggestions to those who are desirous of comfort, to those who are hurting and suffering because of pain and grief. Here is comfort, consolation, and, above all, hope for hearts.

To begin again, what happens to us at the time of death? This can be best defined as the period of time between death of the physical body and the resurrection of it by God.

SLEEP

It is interesting to note that the definition of cemetery refers to sleeping. Different definitions of this word can be a graveyard, a sleeping place, or, more interestingly, a dormitory! Furthermore it means to put to sleep, to lie down, to lie, or to rest. It is implied that a cemetery is a home, a house, or a dwelling. The Hebrew word "sheol" that we find in the Bible is defined as the "abode of the dead." Sheol could simply be a graveyard. Perhaps it is the prison that is spoken of in scripture. Certainly it is not some geographical location in some other plane, or outside of the earth, or in the sky.

Some translations of the Bible will use the word "death" instead of "sleep," but this is contrary to some portions of scripture where the underlying Greek supports the word "sleep." This happens in the translation called the New Revised Standard Version.

In looking at the following verses, notice the Greek words in the first two three pericopes have the same stem for "asleep" and were translated correctly. The stem or lemma is κοιμάω, and it means "to be dead, sleep, fall asleep, die, and pass away."[2]

MATTHEW 27:52:
*The tombs also were opened, and many bodies of
the saints who had fallen asleep (Gk, κεκοιμημένων)
were raised.*

JOHN 11:11:
*After saying this, he told them, "Our friend Lazarus
has fallen asleep (Gk, κεκοίμηται), but I am going
there to awaken him."*

However, it is interesting to note that when Paul writes about Jesus dying he does not use the word sleep. He uses the Greek word for dead (Gk, ἀποθνήσκω).[3] That is why in the 1 Thessalonians example the only one who "died" is Jesus Christ while the others have fallen asleep. In addition, Paul uses another word, in Greek, καθεύδω, which also means to be dead or sleep.[4]

1 THESSALONIANS 5:10:
*[Jesus Christ] who died (Gk, ἀποθανόντος) for us,
so that whether we are awake (Gk, γρηγορῶμεν) or
asleep (Gk, καθεύδωμεν) we may live with him.*

2. Bauer, Danker, Arndt, and Gingrich (BDAG), 3rd ed., 551.

3. BDAG, 3rd ed., 111.

4. BDAG, 3rd ed., 490.

In these following pericopes, we see that the English has been translated as dead, when, in reality, it should be translated as sleeping. Notice that the Greek stem is the same.

Acts 7:60:

Then he knelt down and cried out in a loud voice, "Lord, do not hold this sin against them." When he had said this, he died (Gk, ἐκοιμήθη).

Acts 13:36:

For David, after he had served the purpose of God in his own generation, died, (Gk, ἐκοιμήθη) was laid beside his ancestors, and experienced corruption;

1 Corinthians 11:30:

For this reason many of you are weak and ill, and some have died. (Gk, κοιμῶνται)

1 Corinthians 15:6:

Then he appeared to more than five hundred brothers and sisters at one time, most of whom are still alive, though some have died. (Gk, ἐκοιμήθησαν)

1 Corinthians 15:18:

Then those also who have died (Gk, κοιμηθέντες) in Christ have perished.

1 Corinthians 15:20:

But in fact Christ has been raised from the dead (Gk, νεκρῶν) the first fruits of those who have died. (Gk, κεκοιμημένων)

1 Corinthians 15:51:

Listen, I will tell you a mystery! We will not all die (Gk, κοιμηθησόμεθα), but we will all be changed . . .

2 PETER 3:4:

and saying, "Where is the promise of his coming?
For ever since our ancestors died, (Gk, πατέρες
ἐκοιμήθησαν "fathers fell asleep") all things continue
as they were from the beginning of creation!"

In the following particular pericope Paul is speaking about
the death of Jesus and those who have fallen asleep. In verse 11,
Paul speaks of those who have fallen asleep in Christ and tells us
to grieve but with hope. Furthermore he tells us that Jesus *died*
and he died such a death, such a gigantic and monumental death
that it covers up completely the death of the believers so we may
be able to speak and say that others have fallen asleep. This is
what gives hope. Due to the death of Christ, we can sleep.

1THESSALONIANS 4:13–16:

13 But we do not want you to be uninformed, broth-
ers and sisters, about those who have died, (Gk,
κοιμωμένων) so that you may not grieve as others
do who have no hope. 14 For since we believe that
Jesus died (Gk, ἀπέθανεν) and rose again, even so,
through Jesus, God will bring with him those who
have died. (Gk, κοιμηθέντας) 15 For this we de-
clare to you by the word of the Lord, that we who
are alive, who are left until the coming of the Lord,
will by no means precede those who have died. (Gk,
κοιμηθέντας) 16 For the Lord himself, with a cry
of command, with the archangel's call and with the
sound of God's trumpet, will descend from heaven,
and the dead (Gk, νεκροὶ) in Christ will rise first.

2 CORINTHIANS 5:14:

For the love of Christ urges us on, because we are
convinced that one has died (Gk, ἀπέθανεν) for all;
therefore all have died (Gk, ἀπέθανον).

In the Old Testament, Psalm 13:3 speaks of one who "will sleep the sleep of death." In Proverbs 21:16 we read, "Whoever wanders from the way of understanding will rest in the assembly of the dead." Psalm 4:8 reads, "I will both lie down and sleep in peace." See also: Psalm 22:29, Isaiah 29:10, Jeremiah 51:57, and Daniel 12:2.

Scripture tells us when we die we sleep. Therefore we "sleep" when we die. It is a deeper sleep than any we have ever known, much, much deeper than REM. The Bible tells us that we have died, and our lives are hidden with Christ in God (Col 3:3). We are hidden in the presence of Christ, we are asleep in him but we do not have a continued *conscious* existence. It will not be and is not a continued existence that we are able to move up to another plane of existence where we somehow dwell, eat, breathe, talk, see, and the like. There is simply no activity. We are at rest, deep, deep rest. We are resting and asleep, nothing is being done, there is no activity, we are not active in any manner, shape, or form. It is here we encounter much of the common and pastoral language associated with death. "Rest in peace," the "rest of the blessed dead," "grandpa is sleeping," are only but a few comments that have been said and heard. Christ tells us that he is gentle in heart and will give us *rest for our souls* (Matt 11:29).

Furthermore, Psalm 115:17 tells us "the dead do not praise the LORD, nor do any that go down into silence." And again in Psalm 6:5, "for in death there is no remembrance of you in Sheol, who can give you praise?" We read in Ecclesiastes 9:5–6 that "the living know that they will die, but the dead know nothing; they have no more reward, and even the memory of them is lost. Their love and their hate and their envy have already perished; never again will they have any share in all that happens under the sun." We will have no memories, feel no love, hate, or envy nor can we praise the Lord in death. All things will be silent, "For the fate of humans and the fate of animals is the same; as one dies, so dies the other. They all have the same breath, and humans have no advantage over the animals; for all is vanity. All go to one place; all are from the dust, and all turn to dust again." (Eccl 3:19–20).

Christ himself calls death to be sleeping. According to the Gospel of John 11:11ff, Christ says plainly and explicitly, "Our friend Lazarus has fallen asleep, but I am going there to awaken him." This confused the disciples and they thought that if Lazarus was only sleeping, things would be alright for him, as he was not dead. Once again in this short passage, Jesus had to speak plainly and explain to them in verse 14 that "Lazarus is dead."

Another example from Holy Scripture is the little girl whom Jesus raises from the dead (Mark 5:39–42). Some scholars do not use this as a text to explain and understand that death is not sleeping, but use it in other ways. But it does not make any other sense than its plain and simple use of language. Once again Christ refers to death as sleeping and said, "The child is not dead but sleeping." How much more plainly can one make a statement? Here we must believe the child was dead and not "asleep" as we normally think of it, for there was a commotion and people were weeping. They were grieving the death of their little child. They recognized the signs of death and knew this particular child was not asleep or faking sleep like children often do. This crowd recognized her as dead because they even laughed at Jesus for saying she was asleep.

WE ARE SAFE IN OUR SLEEP
AND FREE FROM SIN

In this sleep of death we are safe. We have rest, no more worries, no more pressures, and we have nothing left to fear. Christ in Matthew 10:28 tells us not to fear those who can kill the body, but cannot kill the soul. In Psalm 4:8, the author says that the Lord makes us to lie down in safety. We can rest in our death; assured that our very lives are God's and are in God's hands—not only the life of the child, but the life of the parent as well (Ezek

18:4). God keeps watch over our soul (Prov 24:12) and to be asleep in Christ is such comfort now that we know!

We are free from sin as well. For whoever has died is free from it (Rom 6:7). What comfort it is not to be trapped and bound by sin. We finally have freedom from bondage. The apostle Paul from his letter to the church in Rome stated (Rom 6:1–11):

> What then are we to say? Should we continue in sin in order that grace may abound? By no means! How can we who died to sin go on living in it? Do you not know that all of us who have been baptized into Christ Jesus were baptized into his death? Therefore we have been buried with him by baptism into death, so that, just as Christ was raised from the dead by the glory of the Father, so we too might walk in newness of life. For if we have been united with him in a death like his, we will certainly be united with him in a resurrection like his. We know that our old self was crucified with him so that the body of sin might be destroyed, and we might no longer be enslaved to sin. For whoever has died is freed from sin. But if we have died with Christ, we believe that we will also live with him. We know that Christ, being raised from the dead, will never die again; death no longer has dominion over him. The death he died, he died to sin, once for all; but the life he lives, he lives to God. So you also must consider yourselves dead to sin and alive to God in Christ Jesus.

THOUGH DEAD, WE ARE ALIVE IN CHRIST

When we are alive, that is, walking and talking on the face of the planet, we believe, teach, and confess that God is with us. Therefore, if God is with us and in us when we are alive, as it is his nature to be, then *surely* God must be with us in our death. God will not leave us alone (John 14:18).

God is a God of the living. God is not a God of the dead. In the quote above, we read in the last verse that we are alive to God in Christ Jesus (Rom 6:11). Christ directly tells us in Matthew 22:32 that "'I am the God of Abraham, the God of Isaac, and the God of Jacob'? He is God not of the dead, but of the living." Likewise in Luke 20:38 we read the same thing, but with something added: "Now he is God not of the dead, but of the living; for to him all of them are alive." Paul speaks that even though we are dead in our sin, God made us alive in Christ (Ephesians 4:25). Paul speaks again of this matter in 1 Corinthians 12:21–23 in a future tense, "so all will be made alive in Christ."

So then, all of the dead are alive, for to God they are alive. God remembers us and will not forget us. But to us, our loved ones are not alive, at least not to us right now. We and our loved ones are still dead. However, we are dead; we are asleep, therefore alive in Christ. We will be made alive in the future, in the resurrection, in the not yet, and the not now. But we are asleep in Christ for the time being, waiting safely.

IN OUR SLEEP WE WILL BE ABLE
TO HEAR OUR LORD

There is something of interest here. In our sleep of death, we will be able to hear. As we sleep on our bed in our home, we may sleep soundly. There is no activity, sans our life processes of breathing, our hearts beating, and perhaps our brains dreaming. We have no recollection of things, and we don't really know where we are when we are asleep. Yet, when something out of the ordinary happens, perhaps a prowler breaking a window or a new creak in the house, we are startled. We sit straight up in bed and blink our eyes wide open, which strain into the darkness to see. Our mind is racing, we have heard something, at least we think so, but are unsure what it is.

So it is when we are dead. We do not know where we are. There are no life processes, no activity, no dreaming, for we are simply and ultimately dead. Nevertheless, we will be able to hear. But we will not hear just anything. We will only hear the voice of the Son of God alone and nothing else. In the gospel of John (5:25, 28) we read:

> Very truly, I tell you, the hour is coming, and is now here, when the dead will hear the voice of the Son of God, and those who hear will live. Do not be astonished at this; for the hour is coming when all who are in their graves will hear his voice and will come out.

The young girl in Mark 5:41 was dead. Yet she heard the words of our Lord, "Little girl, get up" and indeed she did; she got up and walked around. Likewise when Lazarus heard Christ say, "Lazarus, come out" (John 11:43), he did. He came out even though his hands and his feet were bound and his face was wrapped by the burial cloths. If Christ did not clarify to whom he was speaking, meaning speaking directly to the little girl and directly to Lazarus, all the people who were dead would have been resurrected right there on the spot. The resurrection would have come early!

WE CAN'T GO TO CHRIST

Though we are alive in Christ, sleeping, it does not mean we "go" to Christ, but that we are with him. The direction is that God comes to us. So God, meaning Christ and the Holy Spirit, comes to us in our death. We do not "go" anywhere like heaven or hell, nor do we "sit on the lap of Jesus." When we die, we don't move, we don't get transported, we don't go anywhere, but rather Christ comes to us. Christ holds us in the palm of his hand; we are safe for we are asleep in Christ.

Jesus tells us that he will not leave us orphaned, which means Christ will not leave us alone, by ourselves, scared, and frightened. He says he is coming to us. In fact he says he is coming to you (John 14:18). He comes to us because where he has gone we cannot go (John 8:21).

Yet in and among all of this talk, we all "go" to one place, for all are from dust and turn to dust again (Eccl 3:20–21). The Holy Bible, through parables taught by Christ, such as the rich man and Lazarus (Luke 16:19–31), depict of and talk about being somewhere when we are dead. Paul, too, speaks of his desire to depart and be with Christ (Phil 1:23). But what does all this mean when I say that we don't or can't go anywhere, but the scripture appears to say something differently and our viewpoints are contrary to one another?

Here are three different sections of scripture verses that at first glance may appear contradictory to my views. There are more than these few, but these seem to be the most straightforward and suggestive about leaving one's body. These are better known than other pieces of scripture relating to these ideas.

The first "troublesome" section comes from a letter the Apostle Paul wrote to the church at Philippi, which we have recorded as Philippians 1:20b–24:

> Christ will be exalted now as always in my body, whether by life or by death. For to me, living is Christ and dying is gain. If I am to live in the flesh, that means fruitful labor for me; and I do not know which I prefer. I am hard pressed between the two: my desire is to depart and be with Christ, for that is far better; but to remain in the flesh is more necessary for you.

The particularly troubling words in this quotation are to "depart and be with Christ." What do these verses mean? How does one read them? There certainly seems to be something going on here about leaving.

In the Philippians pericope, indeed, it seems that Paul is going somewhere. Carefully note the language where Paul says he wants to depart, to be away. To depart does indeed mean to leave. What Paul is leaving is his earthly existence, his life, his flesh, his breathing, his activity as an apostle. Simply and plainly, *leaving is dying*. In that sense he is leaving or going, as he is leaving "life," he has departed from the surface of the earth to six feet under it, buried in a graveyard. Also note that Paul says he desires to "be with Christ." This does not mean that Paul is going to Christ and somehow he is on a journey to Christ. Paul wants to be with Christ, with him, together. And indeed that can be so for upon Paul's death it is Christ who comes to Paul, just as he comes to us in our death. Christ *comes to us* in our death. He is with us in life as he promised, and he is with us in our death. We don't go to him; he comes to us, in the grave, beginning the gathering that is in his nature. We are together with Christ.

Second, we will look again at the writings of the Apostle Paul. This time the quote comes from the letter of 2 Corinthians 5:6–8:

> So we are always confident; even though we know that while we are at home in the body we are away from the Lord—for we walk by faith, not by sight. Yes, we do have confidence, and we would rather be away from the body and at home with the Lord.

The troubling words here are "away from the body and at home with the Lord." Once again it appears that one leaves the body and goes somewhere, like to be at home with the Lord. It also seems there are two "homes," one *in* the body and the other *with* the Lord. What is happening here?

While we are alive, that is, breathing, living, eating, and walking, we are indeed away from the Lord. For the Lord has been resurrected and is no longer "physically" present as he was 2,000 years ago. However, God has not absconded and left us to ourselves. God is present in this world, dwells among us, and lives in our hearts through faith, but not in his physical form that we would recognize him as Jesus. He is therefore away from our "sight" (Gk, εἴδους). He is away from us looking at him by the act of looking or by seeing. He is away from our eyesight, as Paul tells us. We must live in and by faith, not by sight. We have faith in the Lord even though we do not "see" with our pupils and retinas his physical presence. We are then away from the Lord, as Paul was when he wrote this letter.

To be "home in the body" (Gk, ἐνδημοῦντες) is to be among one's own people, dwelling with others, living in their own country. It is to be in one's own home, *at home*, to be in a familiar place.[5] Perhaps another way to say it may be "to be in the body, at or in our home." In this idea, Paul is indeed absent from the Lord, because he is chained to his bodily existence.[6]

To be "away from the body" (Gk, ἐκδημοῦμεν) means that one dies. To be dead is to be away from the body. It is to be no longer a person chained to the bodily existence on earth, but has now fallen asleep in Christ in faith. One no longer dwells in one's own home, nor are they "at home." They are not among one's own people in one's own geographic location known as a country. Again, falling asleep is indeed to be "at home with the Lord" for one has fallen asleep, died, and Christ comes to the person that is no longer at home in the body for now that person is home with the Lord.

Furthermore, Paul has his forward-looking glasses on and is looking to the resurrection that he carries in his heart in faith. Indeed at the resurrection, we will once again "see" the Lord with our retinas and gaze upon Jesus face to face. We will be at home, with one's own people, with one's own new and resurrected body, in the new home of the Lord.

5. BDAG; 3rd ed., 332.

6. *Theological Dictionary of the New Testament* (TDNT), 2:63–64.

There is also another scripture passage that many scholars have looked at and responded to, and have offered their numerous and varied interpretations. This passage comes from the passion narratives and here it is quoted directly from Luke 23:39–43:

> One of the criminals who were hanged there kept deriding him and saying, "Are you not the Messiah? Save yourself and us!" But the other rebuked him, saying, "Do you not fear God, since you are under the same sentence of condemnation? And we indeed have been condemned justly, for we are getting what we deserve for our deeds, but this man has done nothing wrong." Then he said, "Jesus, remember me when you come into your kingdom." He replied, "Truly I tell you, today you will be with me in Paradise."

The last sentence is the troublesome portion here. "Today you will be with me in Paradise." What does that mean? What is Christ saying? Where is paradise? Do we all get to go there? How do we get there?

These words were spoken directly to the thief, a particular person in a particular time in history, like Christ spoke directly to the little girl and to Lazarus. These specific words are not to be taken as spoken to us directly and that somehow they apply directly to each and every one of us.

It may be that Christ "took" the thief directly to heaven in some manner. This would not be beyond the capability of God. Elijah, the Old Testament prophet, in 2 Kings 2:11, was taken to heaven in a whirlwind. One difference between the two examples is that Elijah did not die like the thief did.

However, those words still may be for all of us in some sense. For when we die, Christ comes to us and though we are dead, we are with Christ. Would it *not* be paradise to be with God? We assume it is heaven. But it is not as scripture plainly calls it paradise (Gk, παραδείσῳ) and not heaven (Gk, οὐρανοῖς).

Accordingly, other definitions are a park, a formal garden, or a transcendent place of blessedness.[7]

Therefore one can confidently say that indeed paradise is to be with Christ. So when we are dead, we too, like the thief, are in paradise. Again, do note the language carefully as Christ said to the thief, "you will be with me." Christ did not say to him or give him an imperative such as "go to paradise" as if this is something the thief could do or somehow accomplish, like split apart at death in order to be with Christ.

There also is much debate over the little comma in this sentence (v. 43) and where it is placed. There may or not be a comma placed between "you" and "today" such as "Truly I tell you(,) today" or similarly, placed after "today" such as "Truly I tell you today(,)" with both placements perhaps leading to different interpretations.

In the Greek language this particular sentence reads, "καὶ εἶπεν αὐτῷ· ἀμήν σοι λέγω, σήμερον μετπ ἐμοῦ ἔσῃ ἐν τῷ παραδείσῳ."[8] A literal translation (author's) would read, "And he said to him, amen to you I say(comma) today with me you will be in the paradise."

One way implies that today, before the day is over, immediately, right now the thief is in paradise, while the other implies that I am telling you something right now in your ear, today, and that eventually, at some time in the future a certain something will take place. So the debate is about timing and about when the thief will enter paradise. Either interpretation works within the framework that has been laid out. For either way, the thief is with Christ in paradise. Either way it is Christ doing the doing and not the thief. The thief is the passive recipient of whatever

---

7. BDAG; 761.

8. Aland, B., Aland, K., Black, M., Martini, C. M., Metzger, B. M., & Wikgren, A. (1993, c. 1979). *The Greek New Testament* (4th ed.) (240). Federal Republic of Germany: United Bible Societies.

Christ is doing and remember, the thief died, so he is sleeping in and with Christ in paradise.

Martin Luther also discussed this passage and here is what he had to say:

> But what answer shall we give in regard to the passage in the New Testament (Luke 23:43): "Today you will be with Me in Paradise"? Also regarding 2 Cor. 12:4: "I was snatched up into ParadiseS"? Indeed, I myself, do not hesitate to assert that Christ and the thief did not enter any physical place. In Paul's case the matter is clear when he says that he did not know whether he was in the body or outside the body. Therefore I am of the opinion that in each of the two instances Paradise designates the state in which Adam was in Paradise, abounding in peace, in freedom from fear, and in all gifts which exist where there is no sin. It is as if Christ said: "Today you will be with Me in Paradise, free from sin and safe from death (except that the Last Day must be awaited, when all this will be laid open to view), just as Adam in Paradise was free from sin, death, and every curse, yet lived in the hope of a future and eternal spiritual life." Thus it is an allegorical Paradise, as it were, just as Scripture also gives the name "Abraham's bosom" (Luke 16:22), not to Abraham's mantle but, in an allegorical sense, to that life which is in the souls who have departed in the faith. They have peace, and they are at rest; and in that quiet state they await the future life and glory.[9]

Luther added:

> Where can it be proved from Scripture that Paradise denotes heaven, and that the trees of Paradise refer to the angels? These ideas have been thought up as something most absurd and altogether useless.[10]

9. *Luther's Works (LW)*, 1:88.
10. *LW,* 1:233.

These last two pericopes, Paul wanting to depart and the thief in paradise, are perhaps the most "troubling" pieces we read in scripture regarding this issue. Luther in his own time had to deal with questions about them as well. It is my view it is because of these two passages that people's individual and personal theology are pushed when they are under duress. Both of these passages are in regard to death, and they are the ones people turn to when they are facing death in some manner, whether of themselves or a loved one. In fact, one of these passages has to do with the very person of Christ, and being involved very deeply, meaning his crucifixion and death, there simply is no better place to turn for help. It is these small contextual pieces of scripture that people seek out and grab onto for comfort after losing their objectivity and being swallowed up in anxiety.

Simply put, we are not divisible, because Christ is not divisible. We cannot split apart, as Christ did not split apart. If the God/man did not split, how is it that we humans can? But honestly, truly, rationally, why is it that we think we that we can, rather, that we think are *capable* enough to split apart at death? When one is alive in life, that is, breathing, moving, talking, eating, drinking, or doing, you cannot "split" apart. We have power, as we can do these things in life. One can tell their hand (body) to pick up a pencil, or type on a computer, or pick up some groceries. But when one is dead, they cannot pick up a pencil, type on a computer, or go the local market. There is no power. In absolute fact and reality, there simply is no power at all. How is it, in life, when one has "power," one cannot split apart, but in death, when there is no power and all things have ceased, that one can?

In life, one cannot will oneself to split or divide. A person cannot do this one thing anymore than one can will peace on the world, or end hunger, or add a single hour to the span of life (Matt 6:27), nor can do even the simplest thing of making one hair white or black (Matt 5:36). One can't have a vision, an experience, or a revelation by oneself, manufactured by oneself, or somehow be its cause. The one and only alternative is that it must be God doing these things to the person.

But there are visions, experiences, and revelations. In these experiences, one does not leave or go somewhere. Where would one go? Experiencing them does not necessarily mean that in some manner one is splitting apart, going, or leaving. It may seem that way, it may "feel" that way, but it does not mean it is that way. Even the apostle Paul stated in his revelations that he *does not know* whether he was in the body or out of the body, but that *only God knows* (2 Cor 12:23). In Ephesians 3:3, Paul said "mystery was made known to me by revelation." Who is doing the doing here? It is not us, ourselves. It is God, doing what God does.

> It is necessary to boast; nothing is to be gained by it, but I will go on to visions and revelations of the Lord. 2 I know a person in Christ who fourteen years ago was caught up to the third heaven—whether in the body or out of the body I do not know; God knows. 3 And I know that such a person—whether in the body or out of the body I do not know; God knows— 4 was caught up into Paradise and heard things that are not to be told, that no mortal is permitted to repeat. [11]

Note the word "mortal" Paul uses here. Mortal simply means that we are not immortal. This pericope is similar to the words Paul uses when he says, "depart and be with Christ." Here the language is similar. In or out of the body, but he doesn't know for sure. The experience Paul is having may be like dreaming. One can dream they are in another location. In the state of sleep, people dream. There are dreams that seem so real, they "feel" as if they are indeed reality. But then one awakens and realizes it was a dream. One could even say, whether in the body or out of the body, like Paul, one simply does not know.

11. *The Holy Bible: NRSV*, 2 Co 12:1–4.

Perhaps it may be something like imagination. In our waking state, we can "imagine." One can "daydream." We can be far away and yet present. There are times when looking into someone else's eyes you realize "he is not there."

Our death is the beginning of our resurrection. Christ is beginning to gather us. This is where Christ said how he longed to gather us up as a hen gathers her brood (Matthew 23:37). Where are we? We did not go anywhere, and we really don't know, but we are dead, sleeping in Christ. We are sleeping as he begins the gathering until he completes it in the resurrection. There is no geographic location that we can point to and say there it is, there is where we are. The only thing we can point to and say where we are geographically is the grave. And perhaps that is where we are, but we are in Christ. That means Christ is in our grave too! For God is everywhere, therefore Christ is everywhere. Or is it perhaps we have been buried in his? (Rom 6).

So we die and we sleep in Christ, we do not know, yet we are alive, for God is a God of the living. We have the spirit of Christ in us. We are in Christ, asleep. This sleep is unlike any other sleep. Like death as in sleep, we do not know the moment when we sleep or when we awake. You have experienced sleep in such a manner that when you awoke, you would have sworn that only a few minutes had passed. When you looked at the clock you realize that a full eight hours have passed! It felt as if your head had just hit the pillow. When you go to sleep at night, you feel assured that you will wake up in the morning. So it is when you die, you will wake in the resurrection, unaware of the time that has passed. It will seem as only a brief, short moment.

In life, in death, awake or asleep, like the apostle Paul said, "whether we live or whether we die, we are the Lord's" (Rom 14:8). Indeed, we are the Lord's and we are all alive in Christ, we just don't fully realize it yet.

5

The Nature of Resurrection

THE NATURE OF RESURRECTION

A s there is no nature of resurrection, for it is a noun, a thing, there is no nature as such to be defined. But we can begin at least to describe it. Resurrection means according to Webster, "the act of rising from the dead."

WHAT IS THE RESURRECTION?

Simply, the resurrection is the dead coming back to life. It is people being called forth from their graves like Lazarus to a new life. It is God who does the calling. Most people refer to the resurrection as the eschaton, meaning the final events in the history of the world. It is the ultimate destiny of mankind. It is also called the Parousia and described as the second coming of Christ and the last judgment. Other language surrounding this event we have heard is the "last days," "the end of days," "the day of the Lord," the return of Christ, the end of the world, or, with a bit of a stretch, "left behind."

The resurrection is also our hope. It means comfort to those who suffer and hurt. It is the hope of all hopes, the greatest one ever. Having a resurrection awaiting us means there is no "nothingness to fear." Christ is our future for he is here, now, and he is there, now, waiting for us. This hope means that all our pain, our grief, our sorrows, will be wiped away and our tears will be dried up. This is what we hang on to. We don't hang on to our own stuff for it is fleeting and has no depth. What we hang on to is a promise of God, not one of humans. This resurrection is something that God can do and that God will do and it is a dependable word to count on and to lean on. Here lies great comfort, for it is a promise of God and comes to us from outside of us, entirely independent of our own "inner life."

The Bible says that "for now we see in a mirror, dimly, but then we will see face to face" (1 Cor 13:12). Imagine that, seeing God face to face! Such hope!

Here is a quote from Hermann Sasse, a Lutheran teacher, pastor, and theologian, who summed up resurrection quite nicely:

> The resurrection is the calling of the whole man, soul and body, out of death into life in the Spirit, just as he once was called to existence in the flesh in this transitory world. The resurrection is a new creation.[1]

WHEN WILL THE RESURRECTION HAPPEN?

According to scripture, this will happen on the last day. It will be at the proper and appointed time by God (1 Tim 6:15). In the Gospel of John (6:40), Jesus tells us ". . . that all who see the Son and believe in him may have eternal life, and I will raise them upon the last day."

The signs of this happening are able to be seen and comprehended by the people on earth.

From the Old Testament we get a glimpse of those future days and times of what it will be like from the prophet Zechariah. We read:

1. Sasse, *We Confess*, 20.

> Then the LORD my God will come, and all the holy ones with him. On that day there shall not be either cold or frost. And there shall be continuous day (it is known to the LORD), not day and not night, for at evening time there shall be light. On that day living waters shall flow out from Jerusalem, half of them to the eastern sea and half of them to the western sea; it shall continue in summer as in winter. And the LORD will become king over all the earth; on that day the LORD will be one and his name one.[2]

Christ (in the New Testament) tells us what to watch for at the beginning of this time:

> When you hear of wars and rumors of wars, do not be alarmed; this must take place, but the end is still to come. For nation will rise against nation, and kingdom against kingdom; there will be earthquakes in various places; there will be famines. This is but the beginning of the birth pangs. (Mark 13:7–8)

There are other signs as well. If we read further into the gospel of Mark, Christ gives us a couple more glimpses of what will happen. Here Christ tells us:

> But in those days, after that suffering, the sun will be darkened, and the moon will not give its light, and the stars will be falling from heaven, and the powers in the heavens will be shaken. Then they will see 'the Son of Man coming in clouds' with great power and glory. Then he will send out the angels, and gather his elect from the four winds, from the ends of the earth to the ends of heaven. (Mark 13:24–27)

These are some of the warnings, indications, and signs that will take place before the resurrection. They will let us know that it is close and that Christ is near. Christ tells us that "when you

2. *The Holy Bible: NRSV*. Zech 14:5b–9.

see these things taking place, you know that he is near, at the very gates" (Mark 13:29).

Even though Jesus gives us some warnings, indications, signs, and a couple of tips about the end, we simply don't know when it will take place. Therefore we are not to be deceived by people who claim to know when the end will arrive, for they do not. This makes them false prophets. Paul tells us that he didn't know either for he said "for you yourselves know very well that the day of the Lord will come like a thief in the night"(1 Thess 5:2). Even Christ himself, the very son of God, does not know when the time will be and tells us that explicitly in Mark 13:32–33:

> But about that day or hour no one knows, neither the angels in heaven, nor the Son, but only the Father. Beware, keep alert; for you do not know when the time will come.

The Lord will come after these signs. The apostle Paul describes what will happen to those who have died. We also find comfort in Paul's words as he encourages us further. These scripture verses come from 1 Thessalonians 4:13–18:

> But we do not want you to be uninformed, brothers and sisters, about those who have died, so that you may not grieve as others do who have no hope. For since we believe that Jesus died and rose again, even so, through Jesus, God will bring with him those who have died. For this we declare to you by the word of the Lord, that we who are alive, who are left until the coming of the Lord, will by no means precede those who have died. For the Lord himself, with a cry of command, with the archangel's call and with the sound of God's trumpet, will descend from heaven, and the dead in Christ will rise first. Then we who are alive, who are left, will be caught up in the clouds together with them to meet the Lord in the air; and so we will be with the Lord forever. Therefore encourage one another with these words.

IF THE SOUL LEAVES THE BODY,
WHY IS THERE A RESURRECTION?

This is *the* question surrounding the different issues encountered in the lives of individuals and in the life of a congregation. No matter how one thinks or what one's views are about suffering, death, and resurrection, how does one understand that if the soul leaves, migrates, or goes to heaven and one is sitting on the lap of Jesus in paradise with all of one's senses and faculties, why would one even want to come back to their body? Please God, no, not *this* body! The whole idea of splitting apart at death and then somehow being joined together again with my old body at the time of the resurrection never made any sense. Why would God do *that*? Why would a person even need a body again? After all, they would be in communion with God with all their faculties and senses, and a body would simply slow a person down. Besides, wouldn't it be better to trade in the old version and update to a newer, younger and a much better looking one? How is this to be reconciled? Luther, as usual had something to say about it. The following quote will hopefully help with some understanding regarding this particular issue.

> Thus through hope we are in possession of the first fruits of immortality, as Paul says (Rom 8:23): "We are saved by hope," until its fullness appears on the Last Day, when we shall experience and see the life in which we believed and for which we hoped.
>
> The flesh has no understanding of this. Its conclusion is that man dies like a beast. Therefore among the philosophers those who were the most outstanding held the opinion that through death the soul was released and freed from the body, but that after it was released from the dwelling of the body, it mingled with the assembly of the gods and was free from all physical inconveniences. This sort of immortality philosophers have envisioned, although they were unable to arrive at an adequately

supported conviction and defense in regard to it. But the Holy Scriptures teach otherwise about the resurrection and eternal life, and they put that hope before our eyes in such a way that we cannot have any doubt about it.[3]

Furthermore, Luther adds:

Christians, both those who are dead and those who are living, await a resurrection of the dead. Abraham lives too. God is God of the living [Matt 22:32]. Now, if one should say that Abraham's soul lives with God but his body is dead, this distinction is rubbish. I will attack it. One must say, 'The whole Abraham, the whole man, shall live.' The other way you tear off a part of Abraham and say, 'It lives.' This is the way the philosophers speak: 'Afterward the soul departed from its domicile,' etc. *That would be a silly soul if it were in heaven and desired its body!*[4] (Emphasis added)

Luther straightforwardly attacks this idea of splitting apart. The soul does not leave its house upon death. There simply is no leaving, no splitting, no "sitting on the lap of Jesus" upon death. That is philosophy not theology, and it is not Christ-centered. What is Christ-centered, and based upon scripture, is that when we die, Christ comes to us and is with us when we sleep and while we wait.

If we split apart or go somewhere, why do we need to be resurrected? We indeed do not split apart, but, whether we are alive or dead, we await the resurrection. Furthermore, if there is a splitting apart, there is no need to be resurrected. Scripture tells us in plain language and in no uncertain terms there will be a resurrection. It makes good and logical sense that we must wait in death for there are things that will be done and fulfilled by Christ, because Christ is not yet done with us.

3. *Luther's Works (LW)*, 1:33.
4. *LW*, 54:447.

Following are some responses and conclusions to that troublesome question. But now, however, the question has migrated into "Why is there going to be a resurrection and what will happen?" The responses below fall into line with knowing that when we die we are asleep in Christ. These are the things that Christ and Scripture tell us about what we confess in the congregation during worship when we recite the Apostle's Creed and say that we believe in the resurrection of the dead. Going through this process of studying and writing has clarified my thinking while at the same time deepening my understanding of Christ and his word.

These things will benefit you as they bring you comfort. It will bring you faith inside that comfort for Christ said, "I am the resurrection and the life. Those who believe in me, even though they die, will live" (John 11:25). Furthermore, he challenges Martha *and you* and asks all of us quite plainly, "Do you believe this?" (John 11:26).

RESURRECTION

One purpose of the resurrection is to raise our mortal bodies from the dead. From Romans 8:11 we read that Christ will raise us from the dead and give life to our mortal bodies through the Spirit that dwells in us. If then our mortal bodies are to be raised it is by the spirit of Christ that currently resides in us, even though we are dead. Because that is so, we are not re-united with our own soul that has departed. It is not our soul "doing" our own resurrecting; it is Christ's spirit "doing" it to us.

Another purpose in this resurrection of our body is that we must be changed, because flesh and blood cannot inherit the Kingdom of God (1 Cor 15:50). We simply must die. Our flesh and blood must come to a halt. Flesh and *blood* cannot inherit the kingdom of God because scripture explicitly states so. We will become flesh and *bone*. The Lord, after he was resurrected, appeared to the disciples and "He said to them, 'Why are you frightened, and why do doubts arise in your hearts? Look at my hands and my feet; see that it is I myself. Touch me and see; for a ghost does not have flesh and *bones* as you see that I have.' And when he had said this, he showed them his hands and his feet" (Luke 24:38–40, italics added). So the Lord showed the disciples his hands and feet post-crucifixion and post-resurrection. At one point Christ appeared to Thomas post-resurrection and said to him, "Put your finger here and see my hands. Reach out your hand and put it in my side. Do not doubt but believe" (John 20:27). One cannot imagine that the wounds in his hands and side were nasty, bloody, and in need of a doctor or surgery. It would be a frightening and gory mess not at all comforting to the disciples, because the Lord told them not to be frightened. One would imagine his wounds were plainly perceptible and unmistakable to the disciples, for Thomas was able to put his hand in the side of Christ. No one would put their hand into such a wound that was made by a spear if it was really horrible. Although some people today might do such a thing, none of the apostles would, because according to Jewish custom and regulations, they were to remain clean.

Touching a dead body was not allowed for that would make one unclean. Thomas had to overcome this rule in his mind, which would have been difficult. If the wounds were in really terrible-looking shape, and especially if they were bleeding, it would have been even more difficult. The wounds therefore must have been more than simply scars of something long since healed, but were not so terrible they made it difficult for Thomas to touch. Remember, too, that Christ told them to be not afraid. This is why Christ can speak of flesh and bone, and not of flesh and blood.

Life is in the blood (Gen 9:4, especially in Lev 17:11, 14) and he poured out his blood for us (for atonement). Christ died and because of his death and his blood we have life. We receive

Christ's body and blood in the sacrament of the altar for he pours it out and gives it to us. There is life in his blood and he gives us this very special blood, creating life in our death.

Christ himself now has no "need" of his own blood and gives it to us. He does not need it for "life" as we know it, for he gets life from God the father. Remember Jesus too is God and so has the power of life without blood. This will be our new life as well. We will get our life, our animation, our power, our very breath, and movement from God and will not need blood in the resurrection of our body.

The next thing we want to know is what kind of body do we come with? It seems that we are not satisfied with some answers; we must want and have, *all* of them. This causes anxiety of a high enough level that we continue to push our own internal theology to the end. First of all, Paul tells us that we are fools by not understanding we do not come to life unless we die (1 Cor 15:36). He tells us there are different kinds of flesh (human, animal, bird, fish), and different kinds of heavenly bodies and earthly bodies (1 Cor 15:39–40). Therefore when we die, like seed of its own, we grow up so to speak, and we are raised from our earthly body to a spiritual body (1 Cor 15:44), for first comes the physical and then the spiritual (1 Cor 15:46). For this inheritance, we must be changed. We will be changed in a moment, in the twinkling of an eye, at the last trumpet. For the trumpet will be sounded and we will be raised from the dead and become imperishable and immortal (1 Cor 15:53ff). Daniel tells us that in the resurrection we will shine like the brightness of the sky (Dan 12:3).

Our confessions give us a little more insight into what kind of body we will be resurrected to. The reformers hold that "Scripture testifies that precisely the substance of this our flesh, but without sin, shall arise, and that in eternal life we shall have and keep precisely this soul, although without sin."[5] This means

5. *Book of Concord* (BC) 516, *Formula of Concord* (FC), *Solid Declaration* (SD), 1:46.

that we indeed do "need" our human body, our human flesh back after we die. For it is precisely this body, the one we now have, that will be resurrected. It will also be changed into a new spiritual body but retain the things that make us the individual that we are and *were*. Jesus gives us a hint as to this new spiritual body and tells us, "For in the resurrection they neither marry nor are given in marriage, but are like angels in heaven" (Matt 22:30). Christ will transform our body of humiliation, by his power, to be conformed to the body of his glory (Phil 3:20–21).

The resurrection of our bodies will be a final victory for Christ. When we are raised from the dead by Christ's doing, he will have conquered death forever on our behalf. Furthermore, "We know that Christ, being raised from the dead, will never die again; death no longer has dominion over him" (Rom 6:9). "This is will be the death of death, for it will be swallowed up in victory" (1 Cor 15:54).

In this, Paul tells us that we get to talk back to death and say, "Where, O death, is your victory? Where, O death, is your sting?" (1 Corinthians 15:55). We are victorious ourselves over death for Christ has given us this victory and has given us new life in him.

In this new life, our bodies are redeemed and freed from bondage. We have great freedom and all of our chains will be broken. Sin will be gone. Sickness and death will be gone. Even creation itself will be set free from the bondage of decay and will obtain freedom. We will be truly children of God (Rom 8:21–23), because we are adopted by God and will receive an inheritance as a child does from a parent.

Previously God had said that we cannot see him and live. Moses asked to see God and God said that he would show himself to Moses but that, "you cannot see my face; for no one shall see me and live" (Exod 33:20). So Moses got to catch only a glimpse of the "back side" of God. For God said, "then I will take away my hand, and you shall see my back; but my face shall not be seen" (Exod 33:23). Later in the New Testament we read that God alone has immortality and dwells in light, whom no one has ever seen or can see (1 Tim 6:16).

In the resurrection, all this changes and we will be able, indeed, we will be privileged and blessed enough, to see God face to face (BC, 567). At that time, God will no longer be hidden from our view. In the resurrection, we are told, "They will see his face, and his name will be on their foreheads" (Rev 22:4). Jesus himself tells us that "In a little while the world will no longer see me, but you will see me; because I live, you also will live" (John 14:19). Again Jesus speaks to us and says, "Blessed are the pure in heart, for they will see God" (Matt 5:8). In the Old Testament we find that when we awake from our sleep of death, we will see God's face and see God directly. In Psalm 17:15 we read, "As for me, I shall behold your face in righteousness; when I awake I shall be satisfied, beholding your likeness."

In life as in death, we follow Christ, for he is the first fruits (1 Cor 15:20). His path is essentially our life and we are to follow in his footsteps. This does not mean that he is our model, something that we have to live up to and become. We know we cannot do that, but rather our life "follows" his life. Our life is similar in that we, too, must pick up our cross (Matt 10:38; 16:24), must suffer and must die (Matt 17:9; 12. 20:18; 26:2; Mark 8:31, etc.). We are afflicted in every way, crushed, persecuted, forsaken, but we will not be overcome by these things. These things are the death of Jesus so that his life can be seen in our bodies (2 Cor 4:7–11). Just like Christ was put to death in the flesh (1 Pet 3:18), we too must die for our bodies are to be put to death so the sin in our bodies might be destroyed (Rom 6:6–7). Like Christ, we too will be resurrected to new life after all these things.

The resurrection is a fulfillment of promises to us by God (Ps 12:6, 18:30, 77:8, 119:41; Luke 24:49; Acts 13:34; Rom 4:16; 2 Cor 7:1; Eph 1:14, etc). God has made many promises to us, including that of raising us up to new life (Rom 6). What other promise is as dependable as one made by God? Humanly promises constantly fail for we all make promises that we cannot or will not keep. God does not do this. His promises will be kept, as they have been, as they are now, and as they will be.

In the resurrection, we will be totally gathered with Christ. This he wants to do like a hen that gathers her brood (Matt 23:37). He has a plan to do this at the proper time, which is the fullness of time, to gather up all things in him and to him, things in heaven and earth and this includes us (Eph 1:10; 2 Thess 2:13; Matt 3:12, 24:31). This means that we will be gathered into his presence (2 Thess 2:1; 2 Cor 2:17; 4:14; 2 Tim 4:1). Once we are in his presence, we will live with him in eternal life (Matt 19:29, 25:46; Luke 18:30; John 3:16, etc.)

The last piece of resurrection is the theme of judgment and repayment. This is where we have heard the words "the great and terrible day of the Lord" (Joel 2:11, 2:31; Zeph 1:18; Mal 4:5). This is all the stuff that Jenkins and LaHaye have written about in *Left Behind,* their imaginative, but not theologically and scripturally correct, *fictional series* about these last days.

Scripture tells us these days are about repayment. God tells us that "Vengeance is mine, I will repay" (Rom 12:19; Heb 10:30; Deut 32:35; Ps 94:1; Isa 34:8; etc.). This is finally where all the scales of justice will be balanced in some manner or form. But we must keep in mind that thinking like this is more humanly than Godly. For God has given us such radical grace that it wipes out a sense of our internal and humanly "justice."

Nevertheless, God tells us he will repay. But we think this is only about evil people and evil deeds, especially what *those people have done to us* in those deeds when we were merely innocent victims. This is the balance or the justice that we all hope for and which seems to be built into our fabric. This repayment is for the good people and the good deeds as well. We seem to forget that at times. Christ tells us in Matthew 16:27 that when he comes "with his angels in the glory of his Father, and then he will repay everyone for what has been done." This includes everyone, you and me, those who have done good as well as those who have done evil. That verse has quite the double meaning to it! But if we need more clarity and explanation, Jesus also tells us to "not be astonished at this [resurrection]; for the hour is coming when all who are in their graves will hear his voice and will come out—those who have done good, to the resurrection of life, and those who have done evil, to the resurrection of condemnation" (John 5:28–29).

God is coming again for final judgment (2 Cor 5:10). We recite this part of the Apostle's Creed in worship as well. We say, "he will come again to judge the living and the dead." God will indeed judge us all and it doesn't matter if we are alive or dead. God will call out the dead to the resurrection while simultaneously dealing with those who are still alive when Christ comes again. Our confessions tell us:

> It is also taught among us that our Lord Jesus Christ will return on the last day for judgment and will raise up all the dead, to give eternal life and everlasting joy to believers and the elect but to condemn ungodly men and the devil to hell and eternal punishment.[6]

There is then a division of the people. Some will be with Christ and others will not. Some will be rewarded and gathered in Christ (Isa 40:10–11), others will be rewarded in a different way—by eternal death. Christ is to be the judge. He will sit on the throne of his glory and separate people one from another, like a shepherd separates the sheep from the goats. Christ will decide who will go away to eternal punishment and who will go into eternal life (Matt 25:31–32, 46). Furthermore in Daniel 12:2, in a prophecy written before the birth of Christ, we know that "many of those who sleep in the dust of the earth shall awake, some to everlasting life, and some to shame and everlasting contempt."

6. *Augsburg Confession (CA)*, Article 17, 38.

In the book of Revelation, there is much symbolism regarding these last days. The book is difficult to "interpret" due to the richness of its symbolism. Here is what the author saw and reports back to us regarding these last days. I will leave the "interpretation" to you:

> Then I saw a great white throne and the one who sat on it; the earth and the heaven fled from his presence, and no place was found for them. And I saw the dead, great and small, standing before the throne, and books were opened. Also another book was opened, the book of life. And the dead were judged according to their works, as recorded in the books. And the sea gave up the dead that were in it, Death and Hades gave up the dead that were in them, and all were judged according to what they had done. Then Death and Hades were thrown into the lake of fire. This is the second death, the lake of fire; and anyone whose name was not found written in the book of life was thrown into the lake of fire. (Rev 20:11–15).

6

The Conclusion

THE PERSONAL theologies of people who believe that humans split apart at death are reacting to their emotions. They are feeling deep and profound anxiety, grief, stress, and duress. In this difficult time of death one must find, or at least attempt to find, comfort and relief from those feelings. In the attempt to do that, we simply make up our own personal theology to bring comfort and, to do so, we push it to the end. The end is nothing else than God. There is nothing greater, larger, or more than Christ. There is nothing further down the road, hidden for us to grope for. The end of the road is Christ; there are no detours, forks, or left turn lanes, only the dead end. There is nothing "beyond" or "past" that in our life, our thinking, or anything we can imagine other than God to push our theology to. That is the best of the best for comfort.

We do not split apart as in our soul or spirit separating from our earthly body. There is no scriptural proof of us going to God at the moment of death or leaving just a little before we die. We do not split apart, leaving our body behind in the grave. We do not go anywhere to "sit on the lap of Jesus." The God/man himself does not split apart, therefore neither can we. If this were so, we would read in scripture about God somehow reuniting our body and soul at the time of the resurrection or, for that matter, at any other time pre- or post-resurrection. Again, if we did split apart, then certainly there would be no need for a bodily resurrection. But this is not so as according to God's word there indeed will be a resurrection. God will raise us from the dead, take us up out of the grave, and give us new life. If there is to be any putting back together, it will be then and only then. This will not be in a sense of re-uniting our split body/soul, but perhaps in a sense of "fixing" or making our bodies whole again and they will be perfect. Even though we may be missing pieces and parts, it does not matter, for God will make all things new. God will transform, change, or as Luther would put it, *translate* our bodies into a spiritual one.

When we die, we sleep the sleep of death. Christ comes to us and is with us in our death, as he is with us in our life. We are "under guard" by Christ who keeps watch over us. We sleep in Christ such a deep sleep there is no dreaming or any other activity. In death, nothing remains except our hearing. However, we will hear only the voice of God alone and nothing else. When God calls our name we will come out of our graves, go through something called the judgment and as believers in Christ receive a new translated spiritual body and live forever, immortal, in eternal life with the living God. We will be in God's presence and see God face to face.

God alone does the resurrection of our bodies and all of creation, with no help by us or from us; we don't co-create any of this. We have no power. We are like receptacles who receive these things from God passively. God is not helped by us in the splitting apart of our body and soul, for we do not split apart. God alone is responsible, because God alone has the power to do what He says. The reformers have written in our confessions:

> For the conversion of our corrupted will, which is noth-
> ing else but a resurrection of the will from spiritual
> death, is solely and alone the work of God, just as the
> bodily resurrection of the flesh is to be ascribed to God
> alone, as was thoroughly demonstrated above from clear
> passages of Holy Scripture.[1]

1. Book of Concord (BC) 538, Formula of Concord (FC), Solid Declaration (SD), Art. 2, par. 87.

In the meantime, whether we are alive or dead, we wait for the coming of the Lord in power and glory. We live in life, in Christ's hands, waiting for the resurrection. We rest in death, in Christ's hands, waiting for the resurrection. Christ has not yet completed and fulfilled all of his promises, which is why we wait. We wait then for the fulfillment of these things, which, in turn, gives us hope for the future. However, just because we are waiting does not mean God isn't doing anything. God is at work on his goals and will complete them. Once again our confessions tell us:

> This, then, is the article which must always remain in force. Creation is past and redemption is accomplished, but the Holy Spirit carries on his work unceasingly until the last day. For this purpose he has appointed a community on earth, through which he speaks and does all his work. For he has not yet gathered together all his Christian people, nor has he completed the granting of forgiveness. Therefore we believe in him who daily brings us into this community through the Word, and imparts, increases, and strengthens faith through the same Word and the forgiveness of sins. Then when his work has been finished and we abide in it, having died to the world and all evil, he will finally make us perfectly and eternally holy. We now wait in faith for this to be accomplished through the Word.[2]

Luther also spoke of this waiting directly and gives us a glimpse of his thinking that our new life will be better than Adam's life in Paradise. But we still wait …

> And so we now wait for the restoration of all things, not only of the soul but also of the body, because on that Day we shall have a better and statelier one than the one in Paradise was. For we shall not be placed into a physical life, which by its nature is subject to change, but into a spiritual life, into which Adam, too, would have been

2. BC 419, Large Catechism (LC) par. 61.

translated if he had lived without sin. To this hope we
are led by Christ, who has restored our freedom from
guilt through the remission of sins and who makes our
state better than the state of Adam was in Paradise.[3]

What do we do? Do we simply wait? Is that what life is,
waiting? That makes life seem useless today, right now, if our life
is nothing but waiting. Our life is not useless, for there is much
here for us to do, such as serve our neighbor. Today, Christ is in
us, dwelling in us, dwells among us, giving us purpose, love, and
forgiveness. Yet our lives are still full of stubbornness and rebel-
lion, along with faith, love, comfort, and especially hope *from our
Lord and Savior, Jesus Christ*. Our confessions, too, give us hope
and they tell us that the Holy Spirit is in us and gives us such
great life:

> For the Old Adam [*Luther's way of saying our "bad" na-
> ture*], like an unmanageable and recalcitrant donkey, is
> still a part of them and must be coerced into the obedi-
> ence of Christ, not only with the instruction, admoni-
> tion, urging, and threatening of the law, but frequently
> also with the club of punishments and miseries, until
> the flesh of sin is put off entirely and man is completely
> renewed in the resurrection. There he will no longer
> require either the preaching of the law or its threats
> and punishments, just as he will no longer require the
> Gospel. They belong to this imperfect life. But just as
> they will see God face to face, so through God's indwell-
> ing Spirit they will do his will spontaneously, without
> coercion, unhindered, perfectly, completely, and with
> sheer joy, and will rejoice therein forever.[4]

We have sheer joy and can rejoice forever for all are alive
in Christ, whether one is alive or dead. In our waiting, though

3. *Luther's Works (LW)*, 1:100.
4. BC, 568.

we don't always fully realize it, we do have this hope, a sure and steadfast anchor of the soul. There is none better than that of Jesus Christ.

Amen.

7

Preaching Christ as Comfort

COMFORT IS PREACHING CHRIST

A FTER PONDERING what has been written, perhaps it would be helpful to put in a small additional piece for some aid with preaching. This comes from knowing we shouldn't preach to grieving people that their loved one is "sitting on the lap of Jesus" or "playing monster trucks with Jesus" or "playing cards in heaven." What then should we preach?

We should not preach more law to those who are suffering. For those who are suffering are already being crushed under it. They feel the terror, the pain, and the despair of the law and of death. They do not need to hear a preacher pile up the law upon them even more than what they are experiencing in their hearts and minds. They have seen the power and the end of the law for their loved one who is dead. They have seen the sting of sin and the power of the law lying in the casket and being buried in the cemetery. This leaves nothing but terror and certainly no comfort in one's heart.

Therefore we preach Gospel, which means Christ. Jesus, of course, is the center of preaching. It is Christ alone who brings comfort, not the preacher who proclaims that a loved one has left their body and is in heaven. That is simply not true based on scripture, so it is not to be preached. Here are some ideas for preaching with the theology that I have put forward.

The one and only idea is that Christ is to be preached—neither soul detachment nor anything else for that matter. The bottom line of preaching Christ is preaching the gospel. Those suffering, hurting, and looking squarely in the face of death are those who desperately want to hear good news, to hear the gospel. These are the ones who need comfort, not terror.

The following is some language that can "work," meaning this type of preaching will bring someone true and deep comfort when they really, truly need to hear the Gospel of Christ. Some of the following I have personally used, while others I have not. These are merely starters for you to do your own thinking and preaching based on the theology that has been laid out in this treatise.

For example:

"Christ is with your loved one right now. Your husband/wife/daughter/son is being held closely to God and close to God's very own heart."

"Jesus is holding them in the palm of his hand. He has so enveloped them that they are completely surrounded by his presence."

"Jesus has promised to be with us in this life, when we are alive. Why would he not be with us in our death? He is with us here, right now, with those who have lost their loved one. He is with (name) right now like he is with us right now."

"Just like Christ is with us when we are alive, he is with us in our death. God is so very close to us no matter what."

"(Name) has found rest in Christ. (Name) is sleeping right now in our Lord. Our Lord is so very close and so very present with (name). We could even say that (name) is in paradise with him."

"Do you remember falling asleep in your mother's or father's arms when you were a child? Just like that, (name) is asleep in Christ's arms."

"There is sure comfort and sure hope in the resurrection of our bodies. Jesus has promised us eternal life and a new body.

We fall asleep in death and we awake in the resurrection, in a moment, in a twinkling of the eye, and we shall see Christ."

"We will not be left orphaned and alone. Christ has promised this. We are not forgotten, God remembers us, forgives us, and gives us new life."

Those are but a few samples of the type of preaching. They are Christ-centered and they follow the form of Christ doing all the work. I hope these examples give you ideas and some fodder to preach Christ alone for it is him alone who is our hope and our sure and steadfast anchor of the soul.

Bibliography

Aland, B., Aland, K., Black, M., Martini, C. M., Metzger, B. M., & Wikgren, A. *The Greek New Testament* (4th ed.). Federal Republic of Germany: United Bible Societies, 1993.

Arndt, W., Danker, F. W., & Bauer, W. *A Greek-English lexicon of the New Testament and other early Christian literature.* "Based on Walter Bauer's Griechisch-deutsches Wröterbuch zu den Schriften des Neuen Testaments und der frühchristlichen [sic] Literatur, sixth edition, ed. Kurt Aland and Barbara Aland, with Viktor Reichmann and on previous English editions by W.F. Arndt, F.W. Gingrich, and F. W. Danker." (3rd ed.) Chicago: University of Chicago Press, 2000.

Forde, Gerhard. *Justification by Faith—A Matter of Death and Life.* Mifflintown: Sigler Press, 1990.

Kantonen, T.A. *Life after Death.* Philadelphia: Fortress Press, 1962.

Kolb, Robert; Nestingen, James. Sources *and Contexts of the Book of Concord. Martin Luther's Torgau Sermon on Christ's Descent into Hell and the Resurrection.* Minneapolis: Fortress Press, 2001, pp. 245–55.

Luther, Martin. *Luther: Letters of Spiritual Counsel.* Translated and edited by Theodore G. Tappert, Vancouver: Regent College Publishing, 2003.

Luther's Works. Edited by Jaroslav Pelikan and Helmut T. Lehmann. 56 vols. Philadelphia: Fortress Press; St. Louis: Concordia Publishing House, 1955–86.

The Complete Sermons of Martin Luther. (Seven volume set). *Volume 3.1, Sermons on Gospel Texts for the 13th–26th Sundays after Trinity.* Grand Rapids: Baker Books, August 2007.

The Complete Sermons of Martin Luther. (Seven volume set). *Volume 4.2, Sermons on Epistle Texts for Trinity Sunday to Advent.* Grand Rapids: Baker Books, August 2007.

Paulson, Steven D. *Endings and Beginnings, Death and Resurrection.* Dialog, Volume 38, Number 1, 1999, pp. 26–34.

Ratke, David C., editor. *Hearing the Word. Lutheran Hermeneutics. A Vision of Life Under the Gospel.* Minneapolis: Lutheran University Press, 2006.

Sasse, Hermann. *We Confess, Anthology.* Translated by Norman Nagel. St. Louis: Concordia Publishing House, 1999.

Simundson, Daniel J. *Hope for All Seasons.* Minneapolis: Augsburg Publishing House, 1988.

Steinke, Peter L. *Healthy Congregations, a Systems Approach.* Herndon: The Alban Institute, 1996.

The Book of Concord: The Confessions of the Evangelical Lutheran Church. Translated and edited by Theodore G. Tappert. Philadelphia: Fortress Press, 1959.

The Holy Bible: New Revised Standard Version. New York: HarperCollins, 1993

Theological Dictionary of the New Testament. Translated and edited by G. Kittel, G. W. Bromiley & G. Friedrich (electronic ed.). Grand Rapids: Eerdmans, 1964.

WORLD WIDE WEB:
www.christianity.co.nz/life_death7.htm
www.truthaboutdeath.com/history.asp
www.pacinst.com/efh/chapter4/death.html